**Editor:**
Mary Kaye Taggart

**Editorial Project Manager:**
Karen J. Goldfluss, M.S. Ed.

**Editor in Chief:**
Sharon Coan, M.S. Ed.

**Cover Artist:**
Marc Kaslauskas

**Art Director:**
Elayne Roberts

**Associate Designer:**
Denise Bauer

**Imaging:**
Alfred Lau
James Edward Grace

**Product Manager:**
Phil Garcia

**Publishers:**
Rachelle Cracchiolo, M.S. Ed.
Mary Dupuy Smith, M.S. Ed.

# Writing *Grants*

## A Complete Guide for Educators

**Author:**
Julia Jasmine, M.A.

*Teacher Created Materials, Inc.*
P.O. Box 1040
Huntington Beach, CA 92647
**ISBN-1-57690-080-0**

©1996 Teacher Created Materials, Inc.          Made in U.S.A.

# Table of Contents

# Introduction

## Money, Money, Money

Teachers probably write more proposals for grants than any other group of people in the United States. Just the idea of a grant presents a tempting prospect. New computers! New software! New books! Money, money, money! Money looks very good indeed when many districts and even states have seen regular funds dry up and disappear.

## You Cannot Get Funded If You Do Not Apply

Certainly, a great deal of money is available from a great many sources, and (as everyone will be glad to tell you) you cannot get funded if you do not apply! Nevertheless, the needs are increasing, the competition is intense, and the work involved in just writing the grant proposal sometimes appears to be overwhelming.

## It Used to Be Easier

Individuals used to write grant proposals with a minimum of preparation. They had needs (or maybe just *wants*), heard about something that was available, got an application form, wrote down a great deal of redundant information couched in the current educational jargon, mailed it off, and waited.

If they were funded, they swung into action and put their project into operation. By the time they were up and running, the educational emphases might have shifted. Very often they were surprised to find that there were no grant funds for the second year and very little interest and support from their administrators or the other teachers in their schools. There was probably a new focus, and they needed or wanted something entirely different anyway.

## Today's Grants for Education

People who write today's grant proposals are much more sophisticated. They are using advanced models to identify their needs, building on programs that are already in place, backing their proposals with unimpeachable statistics, locating multiple sources for funding alternatives as well as for matching funds, and rewriting and reapplying when necessary.

They are almost always part of a team that is committed to the project for a significant period of time. They may form a partnership with other teachers or other schools. They may seek funding from the district level. They call in outside experts to help them get started, to check their works for flaws, and to edit the written documents. These are the people for whom this book is written.

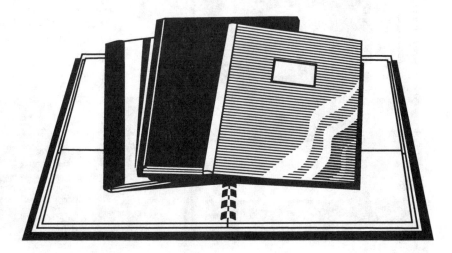

## Grants for Individuals

People today are also applying for grants that affect them personally and promise to enrich their own lives. Teachers, who hesitate to encumber themselves with the debts they can incur while studying for higher degrees, still want to advance on their district's salary schedules. The same dilemma—financial demands on the one hand and career advancement on the other—affects professionals in a variety of fields.

Other people would like to explore their talents and do major work in the arts; still others have ideas for projects that would impact their communities, or even the world, especially in the areas of the environment or ethnic understanding. These are also people who will benefit from this book. Although government grants are not as easy to find in these areas, there is still money out there in these and many other areas from sources such as privately funded foundations. Most of the same skills and much of the same information applies to writing these alternative kinds of grant proposals.

## Transfer Your Skills

In addition, the writing and organizational skills necessary for putting together a grant proposal are also invaluable for writing and putting together the kinds of projects and portfolios that are often demanded in advanced degree programs and as part of the application process for certification by boards such as the National Teacher's Certification program. Once you have written a grant proposal, nothing else seems as hard as it once did.

# Grants for Schools—Part One

## Table of Contents

## Grants for Schools—Part One

# Getting Started

## Which Comes First?

### The Chicken or the Egg?

No, not the chicken or the egg—rather, the *need* or the *grant*. If you have already identified an urgent need in your classroom, school, or district, you know what came first. But, if you hear of a grant that is available, you may decide that you can discover (or even manufacture) a need to fit it.

### A Lucky Result

This approach may sometimes yield a lucky result as you identify an exact match between the purpose of the grant and a glaring need that you had not realized could be addressed in this way. And, if you have some extra time on your hands, it certainly cannot hurt to try. You might get funded. At the very least, you will get some practice in grant writing.

### Build Bridges, Not Roadblocks

Realistically, however, this approach runs into some major roadblocks along the way that a proposal based on a generally perceived need can usually avoid. Below are three of the reasons why it may be more beneficial to apply for grants which request support for needs which have already been identified.

❖ A grant proposal in response to a generally perceived need will have the necessary grass roots support that an off-the-top-of-your-head idea will never be able to gather.

A good grant proposal depends on the support that has built up in your school (or your district) and community in response to a deeply felt need. You are going to have to have a cadre of supportive people: people who will analyze the application, gather data, write, read, and edit. You may need people who will be willing to search out matching funds.

Most importantly, if you do get funded, you will need people who are committed to the day-by-day, nitty gritty of implementing the plan. You do not want people who will congratulate you and then go away. You want people who are so immersed in the proposal that they are dedicated to its success.

❖ The underlying philosophy of the funder will have an impact on your success. If you have really thought out the reason for seeking a grant, you will understand your own educational stance well enough that you will not waste your time applying for a grant that is not a match in this area. Conversely, if you do have a match in philosophy, your well thought out idea will reflect and express this.

❖ If you really need something in your school or district, chances are good that you will have already started with what you have. You probably have the nucleus of a program in place and great plans for going further with what you are doing, *if* you can just get the necessary funds.

# Getting Started

## Which Comes First? *(cont.)*

### Build Bridges, Not Roadblocks *(cont.)*

This is the kind of grant proposal that is getting funded. People who have not at least started with what they have are not considered good prospects. People who want something so much that they are doing what they can do are considered winners.

### Another Way to Look at It

There is another way to look at it, however. Which comes first—the grant or the planning? It is quite possible to do a lot of general planning before you ever think of applying for a particular grant. If you choose to do your planning well in advance, you will always be ready if something you want to apply for comes along.

### Ready for Anything

Complete the following steps toward getting started, and you will be well on your way and ready for anything.

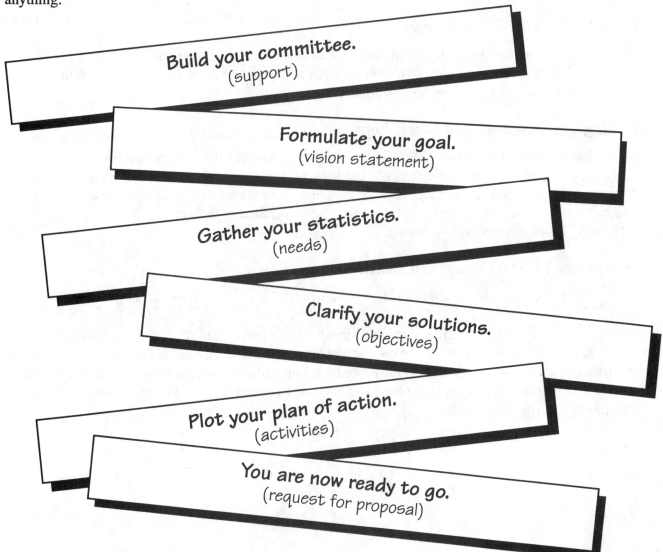

Build your committee.
(support)

Formulate your goal.
(vision statement)

Gather your statistics.
(needs)

Clarify your solutions.
(objectives)

Plot your plan of action.
(activities)

You are now ready to go.
(request for proposal)

# What Is Out There to Help Me?

## Seminars and Workshops

### How Do You Learn Best?

When you begin to look for help in grant writing in general or in writing one particular grant you want to apply for, consider your own learning style. If you like to attend seminars and workshops, there are many to consider. Rather than choosing one from a list of options, think about going to several, or have people on your staff or grant committee attend different ones and share what they learned with everyone. There is always more than one way to look at things.

### What to Look for in the Presenter

Before you sign up for a seminar or workshop, take a look at the background of the person who is giving it. Catalogues or advertising brochures usually list the academic accomplishments of the presenter. Does he or she teach somewhere? Make a phone call. Has he or she written one or more books? Get a copy and take a look at it. Has he or she given other presentations locally? Talk to someone who has attended one. Has he or she actually written a grant that was funded? How long ago? Up-to-date information is important and grant writing has changed.

### What to Look for in the Content

Find out if you will actually write a grant proposal as part of the workshop. Will you read and score the grants written by other people? Will you be given materials to take home with you? Will the presenter be available for personal follow-up help?

### Finding the Seminars and Workshops

Check your mailbox at school and keep your eyes open for brochures or flyers advertising upcoming presentations. Call the extension offices of your local colleges and universities and ask about their offerings in the area of grant writing. Call the people in your school district who are responsible for scheduling in-service training and see if grant writing is included in their plans. Sometimes they are just waiting for an expression of interest.

### Making the Most of What You Learn

Ask everyone attending the workshops and seminars to take notes and collect all of the available materials. Then put the materials from each seminar or workshop into a separate folder and keep the folders in the area where your grant committee meets. Each person can fill out a form to keep track of the materials. This will make it easy to compare notes about what you have been learning. (A sample form and a blank to photocopy are included on pages 9 and 10. Keep these forms with the appropriate folders. The person who filled out the form can act as the contact person to answer questions about the materials in that particular folder.

# What Is Out There to Help Me?

## Seminars and Workshops—Sample Form

| This form has been filled in for you as a demonstration of how it might be used. |
| --- |

**Name:** *Frank Brown*

**Position:** *Committee member/parent*

**Seminar/ Workshop:** *Parents as Partners in Proposals*

**Presenter:** *Judd Pierre*

**Contact Telephone Number:** *(201) 555-1234*

**Main Focus:** *This workshop focused on the role of parents in planning programs and writing grants.*

**Materials:** *Lots of handouts (on shelf in committee meeting room)*

**Evaluation:** *This was really relevant. More of us should go the next time he speaks. In the meantime, I'll try to answer committee members' questions.*

# What Is Out There to Help Me?

## Seminars and Workshops—Blank Form

Make copies of this form for committee members to use when they attend seminars and workshops.

Name: _____

Position: _____

Seminar/
Workshop: _____

Presenter: _____

Contact
Telephone
Number: _____

Main Focus: _____

_____

_____

Materials: _____

_____

Evaluation: _____

_____

_____

_____

# What Is Out There to Help Me?

## Grant Funding Information Centers

### The Foundation Center

The Foundation Center is an independent national service organization. It was established by foundations to provide an authoritative source of foundation and corporate giving. Although the most comprehensive reference collections are in Atlanta, Cleveland, New York, San Francisco, and Washington D.C. Cooperative Collections are located in libraries, community foundations, and other nonprofit agencies throughout the fifty states.

The collections vary in their hours, materials, and services so it is recommended that you call before visiting one of these locations. For new locations or current information the toll-free information number is 1-800-424-9836. The Web site is http://fdncenter.org/library/library.html.

---

## The Main Reference Collections

**Foundation Center**
8th Floor
79 Fifth Avenue
New York, NY 10003
(212) 620-4230

**Foundation Center**
Kent H. Smith Library
1422 Euclid, Suite 1356
Cleveland, OH 44115
(216) 861-1933

**Foundation Center**
312 Sutter Street, Rm. 312
San Francisco, CA 94108
(415) 397-0902

**Foundation Center**
1001 Connecticut Avenue, N.W.
Washington, D.C. 20036
(202) 331-1400

**Foundation Center**
Suite 150, Grand Lobby
Hurt Building, 50 Hurt Plaza
Atlanta, GA 30303
(404) 880-0094

---

## Cooperating Collections

**Alabama**
Birmingham Public Library
Government Documents
2100 Park Place
Birmingham, AL 35203
(205) 226-3600

Huntsville Public Library
915 Monroe Street
Hunstville, AL 35801
(205) 532-5940

**Alabama** *(cont.)*
University of South Alabama
Library Building
Mobile, AL 36688
(205) 460-7025

Auburn University at
Montgomery Library
7300 University Drive
Montgomery, AL 36117-3596
(334) 244-3653

**Alaska**
University of Alaska at
Anchorage
3211 Providence Drive
Anchorage, AK 99508
(907) 786-1848

Juneau Public Library
Reference
292 Marine Way
Juneau, AK 99801
(907) 586-5267

# What Is Out There to Help Me?

## Grant Funding Information Centers *(cont.)*

**Arizona**

Phoenix Public Library
Business and Sciences Unit
12 E. McDowell Road
Phoenix, AZ 85004
(602) 262-4636

Tucson Pima Library
101 North Stone Avenue
Tucson, AZ 87501
(520) 791-4010

**Arkansas**

Westark Community College
Borham Library
5210 Grand Avenue
Ft. Smith, AR 72913
(501) 788-7200

Central Arkansas
Library System
700 Louisiana
Little Rock, AR 72201
(501) 370-5952

Pine Bluff-Jefferson
County Library System
200 East Eighth
Pine Bluff, AR 71601
(501) 534-2159

**California**

California Community
Foundation
Funding Information Center
606 South Olive Street,
Suite 2400
Los Angeles, CA 90014-1526
(213) 413-4042

**California** *(cont.)*

Grant and Resource Center of
Northern California
Building C, Suite A
2280 Benton Drive
Redding, CA 96003
(916) 244-1219

Humboldt Area Foundation
P.O. Box 99
Bayside, CA 95524
(707) 442-2993

Los Angeles Public Library
San Pedro Regional Branch
9131 South Gaffey Street
San Pedro, CA 90731
(310) 548-7779

Los Angeles Public Library
West Valley Regional
Branch Library
19036 Van Owen Street
Reseda, CA 91335
(818) 345-4393

Nonprofit Resource Center
Sacramento Public Library
828 I Street, 2nd Floor
Sacramento, CA 95814
(916) 264-2772

Nonprofit Development Center
Library
1922 The Alameda
Suite 212
San Jose, CA 95126
(408) 248-9505

**California** *(cont.)*

Oakland Community Fund
Nonprofit Resource Center
1203 Preservation Parkway,
Suite 100
Oakland, CA 94612
(510) 834-1010

Peninsula Community
Foundation
Funding Information Library
1700 South El Camino Real,
R301
San Mateo, CA 94402-3049
(415) 358-9392

Riverside City and County
Public Library
3021 Franklin Avenue
Riverside, CA 92502
(909) 782-5201

San Diego Community
Foundation
Funding Information Center
101 West Broadway, Suite 1120
San Diego, CA 92101
(619) 239-8815

Seaside Branch Library
550 Harcourt Street
Seaside, CA 93955
(408) 899-8131

Santa Barbara Public Library
40 East Anapamu Street
Santa Barbara, CA 93101
(805) 962-7653

Santa Monica Public Library
1343 Sixth Street
Santa Monica, CA 90401-1603
(310) 458-8600

# What Is Out There to Help Me?

## Grant Funding Information Centers *(cont.)*

**California** *(cont.)*
Sonoma County Library
3rd and E Streets
Santa Rosa, CA 95404
(707) 545-0831

Ventura County
  Community Foundation
Funding and Information
  Resource Center
1355 Del Norte Road
Camarillo, CA 93010
(805) 988-0196

Volunteer Center of Greater
  Orange County
Nonprofit Management
  Assistance Center
1901 East 4th Street, Suite 100
Santa Ana, CA 92705
(714) 953-1655

**Colorado**
Denver Public Library
General Reference
10 West 14th Avenue Parkway
Denver, CO 80204
(303) 640-6200

Pikes Peak Library District
20 North Cascade
Colorado Springs, CO 80901
(719) 531-6333

**Connecticut**
Danbury Public Library
170 Main Street
Danbury, CT 06810
(203) 797-4527

**Connecticut** *(cont.)*
Greenwich Library
101 West Putnam Avenue
Greenwich, CT 06830
(203) 622-7910

Hartford Public Library
500 Main Street
Hartford, CT 06103
(201) 293-6000

D.A.T.A.
70 Audubon Street
New Haven, CT 06510
(203) 772-1345

**Delaware**
University of Delaware
Hugh Morris Library
Newark, DE 19717-5267
(302) 831-2432

**Florida**
Volusia County Library Center
City Island
Daytona Beach, FL 32014-4484
(904) 257-6036

Nova Southeastern University
Einstein Library
3301 College Avenue
Fort Lauderdale, FL 33314
(305) 475-7050

Indian River Community
  College
Charles South Miley Learning
  Resource Center
3209 Virginia Avenue
Fort Pierce, FL 34981-5599
(407) 462-4757

**Florida** *(cont.)*
Jacksonville Public Libraries
Grants Resource Center
122 North Ocean Street
Jacksonville, FL 32202
(904) 630-2665

Miami-Dade Public Library
Humanities/Social Science
101 West Flagler Street
Miami, FL 33130
(305) 375-5575

Orlando Public Library
Social Sciences Department
101 East Central Blvd.
Orlando, FL 32801
(407) 425-4694

Selby Public Library
Reference
1001 Blvd. of the Arts
Sarasota, FL 34236
(941) 951-5501

Tampa-Hillsborough County
  Public Library
900 North Ashley Drive
Tampa, FL 33602
(813) 273-3628

Community Foundation of Palm
  Beach and Martin Counties
324 Datura Street, Suite 340
West Palm Beach, FL 33401
(407) 659-6800

**Georgia**
Foundation Collection—
Ivan Allen Department
1 Margaret Mitchell Square
Atlanta, GA 30303-1089
(404) 730-1900

# What Is Out There to Help Me?

## Grant Funding Information Centers *(cont.)*

**Georgia** *(cont.)*
Dalton Regional Library
310 Cappes Street
Dalton, GA 30720
(706) 278-4507

Thomas County Public Library
201 North Madison Street
Thomasville, GA 31792
(912) 225-5252

**Hawaii**
University of Hawaii
Hamilton Library
2550 The Mall
Honolulu, HI 96822
(808) 956-7214

Hawaii Community Foundation
Hawaii Resource Center
222 Merchant Street.
Honolulu, HI 96813
(808) 537-6333

**Idaho**
Boise Public Library
715 South, Capitol Blvd.
Boise, ID 83702
(208) 384-4024

Caldwell Public Library
1010 Dearborn Street
Caldwell, ID 83605
(208) 459-3242

**Illinois**
Donors Forum of Chicago
53 West Jackson Blvd.
Suite 430
Chicago, IL 60604-3608
(312) 431-0265

**Illinois** *(cont.)*
Evanston Public Library
1703 Orrington Avenue
Evanston, IL 60201
(708) 866-0305

Rock Island Public Library
401 19th Street
Rock Island, IL 61201
(309) 788-7627

University of Illinois at
Springfield
Brookens Library
Shepherd Road
Springfield, IL 62794-9243
(217) 786-6633

**Indiana**
Allen Co. Public Library
900 Webster Street
Fort Wayne, IN 46802
(219) 424-0544

Indiana University
Northwest Library
3400 Broadway
Gary, IN 46408
(219) 980-6582

Indianapolis-Marion County
Public Library
Social Sciences
40 East Saint Clair
Indianapolis, IN 46206
(317) 269-1733

**Iowa**
Cedar Rapids Library
Foundation Collection
500 First Street, S.E.
Cedar Rapids, IA 52401
(319) 398-5123

**Iowa** *(cont.)*
Southwestern Community
College
Learning Resource Center
1501 West Townline Road
Creston, IA 50801
(515) 782-7081

Public Libraries of Des Moines
100 Locust
Des Moines, IA 50309-1791
(515) 283-4152

Sioux City Public Library
529 Pierce Street
Sioux City, IA 51101-1202
(712) 252-5669

**Kansas**
Dodge City Public Library
1001 2nd Avenue
Dodge City, KS 67801
(316) 225-0248

Topeka and Shawnee County
Public Library
1515 S.W. 10th Avenue
Topeka, KS 66604-1374
(913) 233-2040

Wichita Public Library
223 South Main Street
Wichita, KS 67202
(316) 262-0611

**Kentucky**
Western Kentucky University
Helm-Cravens Library
Bowling Green, KY 42101-3576
(502) 745-6125

# What Is Out There to Help Me?

## Grant Funding Information Centers *(cont.)*

**Kentucky** *(cont.)*
Lexington Public Library
140 East Main Street
Lexington, KY 40507-1376
(606) 231-5520

Louisville Public Library
301 York Street
Louisville, KY 40203
(502) 574-1611

**Louisiana**
East Baton Rouge Parish Library
Grants Collection
120 Saint Louis
Baton Rouge, LA 70802
(504) 389-4960

Beauregard Parish Library
205 S. Washington Avenue
De Ridder, LA 70634
(318) 463-6217

New Orleans Public Library
Business and Science
219 Loyola Avenue
New Orleans, LA 70140
(504) 596-2580

Shreve Memorial Library
424 Texas Street
Shreveport, LA 71120-1523
(318) 226-5894

**Maine**
Maine Grants Information
 Center
University of So. Maine
314 Forrest Avenue
Portland, ME 04104-9301

**Maryland**
Enoch Pratt Free Library
400 Cathedral Street
Baltimore, MD 21201
(410) 396-5430

**Massachusetts**
Associated Grantmakers of
 Massachusetts
294 Washington Street.
Suite 840
Boston, MA 02108
(617) 426-2606

Boston Public Library
Social Science Reference
666 Boylston Street
Boston, MA 02117
(617) 536-5400

Western Massachusetts Funding
 Center
65 Elliot Street
Springfield, MA 01101-1730
(413) 732-3175

Worcester Public Library
Grants Resource Center
Salem Square
Worcester, MA 01608
(508) 799-1655

**Michigan**
Alpena County Library
211 North First Street
Alpena, MI 49707
(517) 356-6188

University of Michigan
Graduate Library
Reference and Research
Ann Arbor, MI 48109-1205
(313) 764-9373

**Michigan** *(cont.)*
Willard Public Library
7 West Van Buren Street
Battle Creek, MI 49017
(616) 968-8166

Henry Ford Centennial Library
Adult Services
16301 Michigan Avenue
Dearborn, MI 48126
(313) 943-2330

Wayne State University
Purdy/Kresge Library
5265 Cass Avenue
Detroit, MI 48202
(313) 577-6424

Michigan State University
 Libraries
Social Science/Humanities
Main Library
East Lansing, MI 48824-1048
(517) 353-8818

Farmington Community Library
32737 West 12 Mile Road
Farmington Hills, MI 48018
(810) 553-0300

University of Michigan, Flint
Library
Flint, MI 48502-2186
(810) 762-3408

Grand Rapids Public Library
Business Dept., 3rd Floor
60 Library Plaza N.E.
Grand Rapids, MI 49503-3093
(616) 456-3600

# What Is Out There to Help Me?

## Grant Funding Information Centers *(cont.)*

**Michigan** *(cont.)*
Michigan Technological
University
Van Pelt Library
1400 Townsend Drive
Houghton, MI 49931
(906) 487-2507

Sault Ste. Marie Public Schools
Office of Compensatory
Education
460 West Spruce Street
Sault Ste. Marie, MI 49783
(906) 635-6619

Northwestern Michigan College
Mark and Helen Osterin Library
1701 East Front Street
Traverse City, MI 49684
(616) 922-1060

**Minnesota**
Duluth Public Library
520 West Superior Street
Duluth, MN 55802
(218) 723-3802

Southwest State University
University Library
Marshall, MN 56258
(507) 537-6176

Minneapolis Public Library
Sociology Department
300 Nicollet Mall
Minneapolis, MN 55401
(612) 372-6555

**Minnesota** *(cont.)*
Rochester Public Library
11 First Street S.E.
Rochester, MN 55904-3777
(507) 285-8002

Saint Paul Public Library
90 West Fourth Street
Saint Paul, MN 55102
(612) 292-6307

**Mississippi**
Jackson/Hinds Library
300 North State Street
Jackson, MS 39201
(601) 968-5803

**Missouri**
Clearinghouse for Mid-continent
Foundations
University of Missouri
5110 Cherry, Suite 310
Kansas City, MO 64110
(816) 235-1176

Kansas City Public Library
311 East 12th Street
Kansas City, MO 64106
(816) 221-9650

Metropolitan Assn. for
Philanthropy, Inc.
5615 Pershing Avenue, Suite 20
Saint Louis, MO 63112
(314) 361-3900

Springfield-Greene County
Library
397 East Central
Springfield, MO 65802
(417) 837-5000

**Montana**
Montana State University,
Billings
Library—Special Collections
1500 North 30th Street
Billings, MT 59101-0298
(406) 657-1662

Bozeman Public Library
220 East Lamme
Bozeman, MT 59715
(406) 582-2402

Montana State Library
Library Services
1515 East 6th Avenue
Helena, MT 59620
(406) 444-3004

University of Montana
Maureen and Mike Mansfield
Library
Missoula, MT 59812-1195
(406) 243-6800

**Nebraska**
University of Nebraska, Lincoln
Love Library
14th and R Streets
Lincoln, NE 68588-0410
(402) 472-2848

W. Dale Clark Library
Social Sciences Department
215 S. 15th Street
Omaha, NE 68102
(402) 444-4826

# What Is Out There to Help Me?

## Grant Funding Information Centers *(cont.)*

**Nevada**
Las Vegas-Clark County
Library District
1401 East Flamingo
Las Vegas, NV 89119
(702) 733-3642

Washoe County Library
301 South Center Street
Reno, NV 89501
(702) 785-4010

**New Hampshire**
New Hampshire Charitable
   Foundation
37 Pleasant Street
Concord, NH 03301-4005
(603) 225-6641

Plymouth State College
Herbert H. Lamson Library
Plymouth, NH 03264
(603) 535-2258

**New Jersey**
Cumberland County Library
New Jersey Room
800 East Commerce Street
Bridgeton, NJ 08302
(609) 453-2210

Free Public Library of Elizabeth
11 South Broad Street
Elizabeth, NJ 07202
(908) 354-6060

County College of Morris
Learning Resource Center
214 Center Grove Road
Randolph, NJ 07869
(201) 328-5296

**New Jersey** *(cont.)*
New Jersey State Library
Governmental Reference
   Services
185 West State Street
Trenton, NJ 08625-0520
(609) 292-6220

**New Mexico**
Albuquerque Community
   Foundation
3301 Menual N.E., Suite 30
Albuquerque, NM 87176-6960
(505) 883-6240

New Mexico State Library
Information Services
325 Don Gasper
Santa Fe, NM 87501-2777
(505) 827-3824

**New York**
New York State Library
Cultural Education Center
Empire State Plaza
Albany, NY 12230
(518) 474-5355

Suffolk Cooperative Library
   System
627 North Sunrise Service Road
Bellport, NY 11713
(516) 286-1600

New York Public Library
Bronx Reference Center
Fordham Branch
2556 Bainbridge Avenue
Bronx, NY 10458
(718) 220-6575

**New York** *(cont.)*
Brooklyn in Touch
Information Center, Inc.
One Hanson Place, Room 2504
Brooklyn, NY 11243
(718) 230-3200

Brooklyn Public Library
Social Sciences Division
Grand Army Plaza
Brooklyn, NY 11238
(718) 780-7700

Buffalo and Erie County
Public Library
Business and Labor Department
Lafayette Square
Buffalo, NY 14203
(716) 858-7097

Huntington Public Library
338 Main Street
Huntington, NY 11743
(516) 427-5165

Queens Borough Public Library
Social Sciences Division
89-11 Merrick Blvd.
Jamaica, NY 11432
(718) 990-0761

Levittown Public Library
1 Bluegrass Lane
Levittown, NY 11756
(516) 731-5728

New York Public Library
Countee Cullen Branch
104 West 136th Street
New York, NY 10030
(212) 491-2070

# What Is Out There to Help Me?

## Grant Funding Information Centers *(cont.)*

**New York** *(cont.)*
Plattsburgh Public Library
19 Oak Street
Plattsburgh, NY 12901
(518) 563-0921

Adriance Memorial Library
Special Services Dept.
93 Market Street
Poughkeepsie, NY 12601
(914) 485-3445

Rochester Public Library
Business, Economics, Law
115 South Avenue
Rochester, NY 14604
(716) 428-7328

Onondaga County Public
 Library
447 South Salina Street
Syracuse, NY 13202-2494
(315) 435-1800

Utica Public Library
303 Genesee Street
Utica, NY 13501
(315) 735-2279

White Plains Public Library
100 Martine Avenue
White Plains, NY 10601
(914) 422-1480

**North Carolina**
Community Foundation of
 Western North Carolina
Learning Resources Center
14 College Street
Asheville, NC 28801
(704) 254-4960

**North Carolina** *(cont.)*
The Duke Endowment
100 North Tryon Street
Suite 3500
Charlotte, NC 28202
(704) 376-0291

Durham County Public Library
301 North Roxboro
Durham, NC 27702
(919) 560-0110

State Library of Government
 and Business Services
Archives Building
101 East Jones Street
Raleigh, NC 27601
(919) 733-3270

Forsyth County Public Library
660 West 5th Street
Winston-Salem, NC 27101
(910) 727-2680

**North Dakota**
Bismarck Public Library
515 North Fifth Street
Bismarck, ND 58501
(701) 222-6410

Fargo Public Library
102 North 3rd Street
Fargo, ND 58102
(701) 241-1491

**Ohio**
Stark County District Library
Humanities
715 Market Avenue North
Canton, OH 44702
(216) 452-0665

Public Library of Cincinnati
and Hamilton County
Grants Resource Center
800 Vine Street, Library Square
Cincinnati, OH 45202-2071
(513) 369-6940

Columbus Metropolitan Library
Business and Technology
96 South Grant Avenue
Columbus, OH 43215
(614) 645-2590

Dayton and Montgomery
 County
Public Library
Grants Resource Center
215 East Third Street
Dayton, OH 45402
(513) 227-9500 ext. 211

Mansfield/Richland County
Public Library
42 West 3rd Street
Mansfield, OH 44902
(419) 521-3110

Toledo-Lucas County
Public Library
Social Sciences Department
325 Michigan Street
Toledo, OH 43624-1614
(419) 259-5245

# What Is Out There to Help Me?

## Grant Funding Information Centers *(cont.)*

**Ohio** *(cont.)*

Youngstown and Mahoning
County Library
305 Wick Avenue
Youngstown, OH 44503
(216) 744-8636

Muskingum County Library
220 North 5th Street
Zanesville, OH 43701
(614) 453-0391

**Oklahoma**

Oklahoma City University
Dulaney Browne Library
2501 North Blackwelder
Oklahoma City, OK 73106
(405) 521-5072

Tulsa City-County Library
400 Civic Center
Tulsa, OK 74103
(918) 596-7944

**Oregon**

Oregon Institute of Technology
Library
3201 Campus Drive
Klamath Falls, OR 97601-8801
(503) 885-1773

Pacific Nonprofit Network
Granstmanship Resource
Library
33 North Central, Suite 211
Medford, OR 97501
(503) 779-6044

**Oregon** *(cont.)*

Multnomah County Library
Government Documents
801 S.W. Tenth Avenue
Portland, OR 97205
(503) 248-5123

Oregon State Library
State Library Building
Salem, OR 97310
(503) 378-4277

**Pennsylvania**

Northampton Community
College
Learning Resources Center
3835 Green Pond Rd.
Bethlehem, PA 18017
(610) 861-5360

Erie County Library System
27 South Park Row
Erie, PA 16501
(814) 451-6927

Dauphin County Library System
Central Library
101 Walnut Street
Harrisburg, PA 17101
(717) 234-4976

Lancaster County Public Library
125 North Duke Street
Lancaster, PA 17602
(717) 394-2651

**Pennsylvania** *(cont.)*

Free Library of Philadelphia
Regional Foundation Center
Logan Square
Philadelphia, PA 19103
(215) 686-5423

Carnegie Library of Pittsburgh
Foundation Collection
4400 Forbes Avenue
Pittsburgh, PA 15213-4080
(412) 622-1917

Pocono Northeast Development
Fund
James Pettinger Memorial
Library
1151 Oak Street
Pittston, PA 18640-3755
(717) 655-5581

Reading Public Library
100 South Fifth Street
Reading, PA 19602
(610) 655-6355

Martin Library
159 Market Street
York, PA 17401
(717) 846-5300

**Rhode Island**

Providence Public Library
225 Washington Street
Providence, RI 02906
(401) 455-8088

# What Is Out There to Help Me?

## Grant Funding Information Centers *(cont.)*

**South Carolina**

Anderson County Library
202 East Greenville Street
Anderson, SC, 29621
(803) 260-4500

Charleston County Library
404 King Street
Charleston, SC 29403
(803) 723-1645

South Carolina State Library
1500 Senate Street
Columbia, SC 29211
(803) 734-8666

**South Dakota**

Nonprofit Grants Assistance
 Center
Dakota State University
Business and Education Institute
3534 Southwestern Avenue
Sioux Falls, SD 57105
(605) 367-5380

South Dakota State Library
800 Governors Drive
Pierre, SD 57501-2294
(605) 773-5070
(800) 592-1841 (SD res.)

Sioux Falls Area Foundation
141 North Main Avenue
Suite 310
Sioux Falls, SD 57102-1132
(605) 336-7055

**Tennessee**

Knox County Public
Library
500 West Church Avenue
Knoxville, TN 37902
(615) 544-5700

Memphis and Shelby County
Public Library
1850 Peabody Avenue
Memphis, TN 38104
(901) 725-8877

Nashville Public Library
Business Information Div.
225 Polk Avenue
Nashville, TN 37203
(615) 862-5843

**Texas**

Abilene Center for Nonprofit
 Management
Funding Information Library
500 North Chestnut, Suite 1511
Abilene, TX 79604
(915) 677-8166

Amarillo Area Foundation
700 First National Place
801 South Fillmore
Amarillo, TX 79101
(806) 376-4521

Hogg Foundation for Mental
 Health
3001 Lake Austin Blvd.
Austin, TX 78703
(512) 471-5041

**Texas** *(cont.)*

Texas A & M University at
 Corpus Christi
Library
Reference Department
6300 Ocean Drive
Corpus Christi, TX 78412
(512) 994-2608

Dallas Public Library
Urban Information
1515 Young Street
Dallas, TX 75201
(214) 670-1487

El Paso Community Foundation
201 East Main Street,
 Suite 1616
El Paso, TX 79901
(915) 533-4020

Funding Information Center of
 Fort Worth
Texas Christian University
Library
2800 South University Drive
Fort Worth, TX 76129
(817) 921-7664

Houston Public Library
Bibliographic Information
 Center
500 McKinney
Houston, TX 77002
(713) 236-1313

Longview Public Library
222 West Cotton Street
Longview, TX 75601
(903) 237-1352

# What Is Out There to Help Me?

## Grant Funding Information Centers *(cont.)*

**Texas** *(cont.)*
Lubbock Area Foundation, Inc.
1655 Main Street, Suite 209
Lubbock, TX 79401
(806) 762-8061

Funding Information Center
530 McCullough, Suite 600
San Antonio, TX 78212-8270
(210) 227-4333

North Texas Center for
  Nonprofit Management
624 Indiana, Suite 307
Wichita Falls, TX 76301
(817) 322-4961

**Utah**
Salt Lake City Public Library
209 East 500 South
Salt Lake City, UT 84111
(801) 524-8200

**Vermont**
Vermont Department of
  Libraries
Reference and Law Information
  Services
109 State Street
Montpelier, VT 05609
(802) 828-3268

**Virginia**
Hampton Public Library
4207 Victoria Blvd.
Hampton, VA 23669
(804) 727-1312

**Virginia** *(cont.)*
Richmond Public Library
Business, Science and
  Technology
101 East Franklin Street
Richmond, VA 23219
(804) 780-8223

Roanoke City Public Library
  System
Central Library
706 South Jefferson Street
Roanoke, VA 24016
(703) 981-2477

**Washington**
Mid-Columbia Library
405 South Dayton
Kennewick, WA 99336
(509) 586-3156

Seattle Public Library
Science, Social Science
1000 Fourth Avenue
Seattle, WA 98104
(206) 386-4620

Spokane Public Library
Funding Information Center
West 811 Main Avenue
Spokane, WA 99201
(509) 626-5347

United Way of Pierce Co.
Center for Nonprofit
  Development
734 Broadway
P.O. Box 2215
Tacoma, WA 98401
(206) 597-6686

**Washington** *(cont.)*
Greater Wenatchee Community
Foundation at the Wenatchee
Public Library
310 Douglas Street
Wenatchee, WA 98807
(509) 662-5021

**West Virginia**
Kanawha County Public Library
123 Capitol Street
Charleston, WV 25301
(304) 343-4646

**Wisconsin**
University of Wisconsin,
  Madison
Memorial Library
728 State Street
Madison, WI 53706
(608) 262-3242

Marquette University Memorial
  Library
Funding Information Center
1415 West Wisconsin Avenue
Milwaukee, WI 53201-3141
(414) 288-1515

University of Wisconsin,
  Stevens Point
Library—Foundation Collection
99 Reserve Street
Stevens Point, WI 54481-3897
(715) 346-4204

**Wyoming**
Natrona County Public Library
307 East 2nd Street
Casper, WY 82601-2598
(307) 237-4935

# What Is Out There to Help Me?

## Grant Funding Information Centers *(cont.)*

**Wyoming** *(cont.)*

Laramie County Community
  College
Instructional Resource Center
1400 East College Drive
Cheyenne, WY 82007-3299
(307) 778-1206

Campbell County Public Library
2101 4-J Road
Gillette, WY 82716
(307) 682-3223

**Wyoming** *(cont.)*

Teton County Library
320 South King Street
Jackson, WY 83001
(307) 733-2164

Rock Springs Library
400 C Street
Rock Springs, WY 82901
(307) 352-6667

**Puerto Rico**

University of Puerto Rico
Ponce Technological College
  Library
Box 7186
Ponce, PR 00732
(809) 844-8181

Universidad Del Sagrado
  Corazon
M.M.T. Guevara Library
Santurce, PR 00914
(809) 728-1515  ext. 4357

### Research Tips

♦ When you go into one of these centers, prepare to be overwhelmed by the amount of material available to you. Plan to visit more than once, if you can. The first time just look around, and the next time do more specific research.

Ask for help. The people who staff these centers are knowledgeable, supportive, and used to researchers who feel totally lost.

♦ If you are not near one of these centers, take a look at what is offered in your local city and county libraries. The reference desk librarian at a central or main branch library can often direct you to shelves full of large volumes of grant information.

♦ Learn to use the computer services of your library. You can often find and download exactly what you need without leaving your chair. Ask someone how to access the system and how to use the printer attached to it. If you need a prepaid card to put into the printer, get it before you start your search. You will not be able to just leave your computer screen to get a card and expect to find your information on the screen when you get back.

Write down the key words you use in your computer search. Cross out the ones that do not work, but keep a list of those that take you where you want to go. (Keep this list in your wallet with your prepaid printer card.) Then you will not have to think through the entire process to get back to your material.

# The Grant Coach

## A Profile

### Like the Athletic Coach

The newest and potentially most useful help a school or a district can obtain for grant writing is the services of a grant coach. The grant coach, like the athletic coach, is an expert in all areas of the "sport," knows what you need to have, get, and do, and can motivate you to get started, keep going, and make a good showing. The grant coach cannot guarantee a win any more than the athletic coach can, but having a good one can greatly improve your chances.

### Different From the Professional Grant Writer

A grant coach is different from a professional grant writer. A grant writer comes into a school or a district and gathers information about needs, objectives, proposed activities, and so on by looking up statistical data and interviewing potential participants. Then he or she writes the grant. But, even if the match between what you want and what is written is a perfect one, and even if the grant is funded, you have lost a couple of very important things: the grass roots support that comes from groups of interested people working together to get something, and the built-in commitment and ownership that grows out of a hard job well done. Basically, if someone else writes your grant, it is not yours anymore.

A grant coach pulls everyone together, helps to form networks and committees, and encourages everyone to play on the same team. He or she helps people dialogue to identify their real needs, appropriate solutions, meaningful activities, and the funding instrument that will best meet these criteria. Then, instead of writing the grant, the grant coach shows the people who are really involved how to do it themselves. Most important of all, the grant coach keeps everyone focused on the task and motivated to finish and succeed. (Picture an athletic coach jumping up and down on the sidelines, waving things and cheering.) In addition, when it is all over, the grant coach will help you put the project into action.

### Ellen Zimet, Grant Coach

"Do these people really exist?" I can hear you asking as you read. Yes, indeed they do. Ellen Zimet is an educational grants consultant with her own company, EZGrants. (See listing on page 240, Resources.) She participates in many activities involved with grants. One of her most interesting roles is acting as a grant coach. Here are her answers to some questions you might want to ask her.

• • • • • • • • • • • • • • • • • • • • • • • • • • • • • • • • • • • • • • • • • • • • • • • • • • • • • • • • • • • • • • • • • • • • • •

*What, exactly, is a grant coach?*

> **Ellen Zimet:** "A grant coach is hard to define exactly. The best analogy is probably an athletic coach, somebody who can teach you the skills you need to know, motivate you, and keep you focused on the task you have undertaken."

# The Grant Coach

## A Profile *(cont.)*

* * * * * * * * * * * * * * * * * * * * * * * * * * * * * * * * * * * * * * * * * * * * * * * * * * * * *

*How does being a grant coach differ from being a professional grant writer?*

**Zimet:** "A professional grant writer takes over the project and produces a finished product (the grant proposal)."

* * * * * * * * * * * * * * * * * * * * * * * * * * * * * * * * * * * * * * * * * * * * * * * * * * * * *

*How did you become a grant coach? What is your background?*

**Zimet:** "My background is mostly in education. I was a secondary principal in the Los Angeles Unified School District when I retired in 1991 with 27 years experience in teaching, counseling, and school administration and started my own grant consulting and project management business. I started writing grant proposals as a teacher and principal."

* * * * * * * * * * * * * * * * * * * * * * * * * * * * * * * * * * * * * * * * * * * * * * * * * * * * *

*What is your track record?*

**Zimet:** "During the past four years the proposals I've been responsible for—sometimes as writer or rewriter, sometimes as coach and editor—have received funding of over $6,500,000.00 for schools and districts throughout the Greater Los Angeles area. There have been 27 proposals, 20 of which were funded and three of which are still pending. I am still involved with several of the funded proposals as a program manager and process evaluator."

* * * * * * * * * * * * * * * * * * * * * * * * * * * * * * * * * * * * * * * * * * * * * * * * * * * * *

*How much do you charge?*

**Zimet:** "I charge a daily rate depending on the work I'm being asked to do. Like most people with a background in education, I have found it hard to 'sell' myself. However, I have found that people only respect what they pay for."

* * * * * * * * * * * * * * * * * * * * * * * * * * * * * * * * * * * * * * * * * * * * * * * * * * * * *

*So your fee is not contingent on funding?*

**Zimet:** "No, it's a flat fee, up front. However, even if a proposal isn't funded the first time it is submitted, it is often funded the next year. And the skills that people acquire when writing a grant are transferable to their next attempt, so they haven't wasted their money."

* * * * * * * * * * * * * * * * * * * * * * * * * * * * * * * * * * * * * * * * * * * * * * * * * * * * *

*Does being a grant coach take all of your time?*

**Zimet:** "It takes a lot of it, but I also give workshops and teach classes. I act as a consultant to an educational video production company and I have written curriculum guides for *The Los Angeles Times* as well as journal articles. Currently, I'm writing a book about successful grant writing."

* * * * * * * * * * * * * * * * * * * * * * * * * * * * * * * * * * * * * * * * * * * * * * * * * * * * *

*How could people find a grant coach in their local areas?*

**Zimet:** "By networking. Go to workshops and talk to the presenters. Call schools and districts that have been successful in getting their proposals funded. Ask about consultants, if people don't know about grant coaches. Or, they can contact me at EZGrants aol.com."

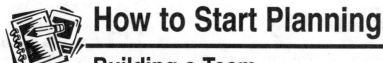

# How to Start Planning

## Building a Team

### A Permanent Committee

It is important to gather together a group of people who will function as a permanent standing committee in your school to work on grants. Ideally, this committee should consist of the principal, the teachers who are able to commit their time, parents, and other members of the community.

There will be some turnover, of course, but a nucleus should remain and the roles should stay the same even if they are filled by different people. If you find your original core group through a survey, have new people complete the survey as they join. In that way you can stay focused and also make adjustments if conditions change. Write many invitation and appreciation letters. This is an area where your principal may be able to lend a hand.

### Help for Individuals

Even those teachers who select to apply for grants as individuals will benefit by the work of this committee which will serve as an information pool as well as a support group. If news of a small grant comes along, a teacher who might not want to invest the time necessary to gather data to back up his or her proposal, could go to the grant committee for this information and for help with editing and formatting.

### The Survey

Put together a survey that will get the results you want. (That sentence is not as "rigged" as it may sound.) Just do not elicit negative feedback by the way you ask your questions.

Phrase the majority of your questions or requests for comment in positive ways. "What new experiences would you like your child to have?" will attract the kinds of responses that will enable you to identify potential committee members. "What is the worst experience your child ever had in school?" will probably not result in a helpful suggestion. However, this negative question could be replaced with a request such as this, "If your child has had a negative experience in school, please describe it and suggest a way that it could have been avoided."

Have a space for comments. That is the place where you will find your critics and, believe it or not, you want some of your worst critics on the committee. They will keep you on the straight and narrow path when you are identifying needs and proposing solutions. Maybe even more importantly, they will be so busy working constructively on the real problems that they will not have time to stir up dissension in the community. People are often negative simply because they feel powerless.

# How to Start Planning

## Building a Team *(cont.)*

### Goal Statements

The surveys are very important because the collected data can point the way toward your goal statements. You will probably come up with a number of them which you can state tentatively and offer for discussion and reworking by the full committee when it is organized. This process makes a good activity for the first couple of scheduled meetings.

### The Roles

One of the first tasks to consider in committee building is the assignment of *roles.* It is more exciting to have a role than just a job.

### The Chairperson

When you first begin to function as a committee, probably one composed of the principal or a designated lead teacher and some volunteer teachers, you will need a chairperson who will coordinate your activities. This person can also be in charge of sending out the surveys and compiling the results. The committee can then decide who to invite to join them and send out the letters of invitation. When people make the commitment to join the committee, they should get letters of appreciation along with a schedule of meetings.

> **How to Start Planning**
> **Building a Team** *(cont.)*
>
> ### School Survey
>
> Fill out this part of the survey if you are willing to sign your name. Otherwise, return the three previous pages to the school office.
>
> 11. Would you like us to contact you to discuss any ideas or problems you might have? _____
>
> 12. In which of the following areas would you be willing to help at school? Please note the times you could be available.
>
> math tutor _____
>
> reading tutor _____
>
> classroom aide _____
>
> computer aide _____
>
> library aide _____
>
> field trips _____
>
> parties _____
>
> fund-raising _____
>
> planning _____
>
> **Name:** _____
>
> **Address:** _____
>
> **Phone Number:** _____
>
> ©Teacher Created Materials, Inc.
>
> *31*
>
> #2080 Writing Grants

### Researchers

As you go along, you will need one or more researchers who will read and share books and articles on the grant writing process. These people are the logical choice to visit the Foundation Centers listed on pages 11-22. They can also condense their information and report it on a handy form. (See pages 46 and 47.)

### Statisticians

You will also need people who like to gather and compile data. They could be called your statisticians. They should collect and keep test profiles, demographics, and all kinds of test scores. Have them count things such as the number and kinds of working computers and printers in your school and who has access to them for what periods of time. If these statisticians themselves have access to computers, they can generate charts and graphs with their data.

# How to Start Planning

## Building a Team *(cont.)*

### Writer

When you get to the point where you are actually writing a grant proposal, you should have one writer so that the entire proposal is written in one style. Everyone on the committee can contribute but the writer should pull together the style.

### Editor

You will need at least one editor, someone who knows quite a lot about grammar, punctuation, spelling, and sentence structure. It is also a good idea to have another editor who reads for content and inconsistencies.

### Critic

Do not forget to have at least one critic, preferably someone who is sensitive to many issues of bias. While almost everyone in education is aware of racial and ethnic bias in the abstract, people sometimes do not recognize them in their own opinions. And, of course, gender bias can still slip in, if just through an outdated use of pronouns.

### Liaison

It is nice to have individuals on your committee who can act as liaisons with other groups—business organizations, service clubs, and your own school's parent organization. Networking can be important, as will be seen when alternative methods of funding are considered.

### Summing Up

Building a team is time-consuming but rewarding. You will not only be ready for anything in the way of a grant; you will have created a base of positive public relations that will make everything you do more constructive and optimistic.

# How to Start Planning

## Building a Team *(cont.)*

Use this survey as is or develop one of your own. Send it to parents and other selected members of the community to elicit feedback and suggest members for your grant committee.

## School Survey

School: _____ Date: _____

Please take some time to fill out this survey about our school and return it to the school office.

1. Do you have children attending this school? ❏ Yes ❏ No

2. **If yes,** please list age(s), grade(s), and teacher(s). Use the back of this page if you need more room.

| **Age** | **Grade** | **Teacher** |
|---------|-----------|-------------|
| _____ | _____ | _____ |
| _____ | _____ | _____ |
| _____ | _____ | _____ |

3. **If no,** please describe your interest in or connection to the school.

_____

_____

_____

4. What do you like best about the school?

_____

_____

_____

# How to Start Planning

## Building a Team *(cont.)*

## School Survey

5. Which existing programs do your children enjoy most?

_____

_____

_____

_____

_____

6. Which existing programs would you like to see expanded?

_____

_____

_____

_____

_____

7. What new experiences would you like your child to have? *(Think big!)*

_____

_____

_____

_____

_____

## School Survey

8. What new equipment do you think our school needs?

_____

_____

_____

_____

_____

9. If your child has had a negative experience in school, please describe it and suggest a way that it could have been avoided or corrected.

_____

_____

_____

_____

_____

10. Use the space below for any comments you would like to add.

_____

_____

_____

_____

_____

_____

# How to Start Planning

## Building a Team *(cont.)*

---

## School Survey

> Fill out this part of the survey if you are willing to sign your name. Otherwise, return the three previous pages to the school office.

11. Would you like us to contact you to discuss any ideas or problems you might have? _____

12. In which of the following areas would you be willing to help at school? Please note the times you could be available.

math tutor _____

reading tutor _____

classroom aide _____

computer aide _____

library aide _____

field trips _____

parties _____

fund-raising _____

planning _____

**Name:** _____

**Address:** _____

**Phone Number:** _____

---

# How to Start Planning

## Building a Team *(cont.)*

Use this form or create a similar one to tabulate the results of your survey. The comments from item 10 on the survey can be copied and attached to this tabulation. Use this information when your committee starts to write goal statements. (Items 9 and 11 on the survey should be dealt with on a personal basis. The information in item 2 is for school use.)

## School Survey Tabulation

1. Range of ages represented: _____

   _____

2. Range of grades represented: _____

   _____

3. People, other than parents, responding to survey: _____

   _____

   _____

4. Things liked the most about our school *(numbers indicate the amount of times mentioned):*

   _____

   _____

   _____

   _____

5. Existing programs most enjoyed by children *(numbers indicate the amount of times mentioned):*

   _____

   _____

   _____

   _____

# How to Start Planning

## Building a Team *(cont.)*

## School Survey Tabulation *(cont.)*

6. Existing programs to be expanded *(numbers indicate the amount of times mentioned)*:

_____

_____

_____

_____

_____

7. New experiences *(numbers indicate the amount of times mentioned)*:

_____

_____

_____

_____

_____

8. New equipment *(numbers indicate the amount of times mentioned)*:

_____

_____

_____

_____

_____

# How to Start Planning

## Building a Team *(cont.)*

Below is an example of how this survey might look when completed.

---

# School Survey—Example

School: *Jefferson Elementary*                    Date: *10-21*

Please take some time to fill out this survey about our school and return it to the school office.

1. Do you have children attending this school?    ☑ Yes    ❏ No

2. **If yes,** please list age(s), grade(s), and teacher(s).  Use the back of this page if you need more room.

| Age | Grade | Teacher |
|-----|-------|---------|
| 7   | 2     | Jones   |
| 12  | 6     | Everly  |
|     |       |         |

3. **If no,** please describe your interest in or connection to the school.

_____

_____

_____

4. What do you like best about the school?

   *All the programs that involve parents.  Tutor Corps is my*

   *favorite.*

---

# How to Start Planning

## Building a Team *(cont.)*

## School Survey—Example *(cont.)*

5. Which existing programs do your children enjoy most?

*My second grader loves math and reading. The sixth grader enjoys science, especially the lab experiments.*

6. Which existing programs would you like to see expanded?

*Science*

*Math*

7. What new experiences would you like your child to have? *(Think big!)*

*More field trips to museums, etc.*

*People from the arts to visit the school.*

*A more up-to-date P.E. program.*

## School Survey—Example *(cont.)*

8. What new equipment do you think our school needs?

*Sports and playground equipment.*

*Software for the computer lab.*

*More computers in the computer lab and the classrooms.*

9. If your child has had a negative experience in school, please describe it and suggest a way that it could have been avoided or corrected.

*My sixth grader is having difficulty with the computer programs—there is never enough time to complete anything. You need more help in the computer lab so that the kids can better use the time they do have.*

10. Use the space below for any comments you would like to add.

*If there is not enough money to staff the computer lab, maybe parents could help.*

# How to Start Planning

## Building a Team *(cont.)*

### School Survey—Example *(cont.)*

> Fill out this part of the survey if you are willing to sign your name.
> Otherwise, return the three previous pages to the school office.

11. Would you like us to contact you to discuss any ideas or problems you might have? _____ *yes* _____

12. In which of the following areas would you be willing to help at school? Please note the times you could be available.

math tutor _____ *already helping* _____

reading tutor _____ *already helping* _____

classroom aide _____

computer aide _____

library aide _____

field trips _____

parties _____

fund-raising _____

planning _____ *I'll arrange time!* _____

**Name:** _____ *Marci McGowan* _____

**Address:** _____ *23 Portola Ave., Anytown, U.S.A. 00000* _____

**Phone Number:** _____ *555-9210* _____

# How to Start Planning

## Building a Team *(cont.)*

This is an example of how to tabulate your survey results.

## School Survey Tabulation—Example

1. Range of ages represented: _5–12 years_

   _Responses from parents of all levels_

2. Range of grades represented: _K–6_

   _Responses at all grades_

3. People, other than parents, responding to survey: _____

   _Ron Jeffrey--School Board_

   _Barkley, S. and J.--Community Partnership_

4. Things liked the most about our school *(numbers indicate the amount of times mentioned)*:

   | | |
   |---|---|
   | Tutor Corps | 20 |
   | Science program | 48 |
   | Friendly attitude | 30 |
   | Teachers | 40 |

5. Existing programs most enjoyed by children *(numbers indicate the amount of times mentioned)*:

   | | |
   |---|---|
   | Science | 50 |
   | Reading | 45 |
   | School play | 70 |

# How to Start Planning

## Building a Team *(cont.)*

---

# School Survey Tabulation—Example *(cont.)*

6. Existing programs to be expanded *(numbers indicate the amount of times mentioned)*:

| | |
|---|---|
| Computer lab | 101 |
| Music | 60 |

7. New experiences *(numbers indicate the amount of times mentioned)*:

| | |
|---|---|
| Cultural events | 55 |
| Field trips | 60 |

8. New equipment *(numbers indicate the amount of times mentioned)*:

| | |
|---|---|
| Computer hardware | 60 |
| Computer software | 101 |
| Playground | 75 |

---

# How to Start Planning

## Building a Team *(cont.)*

### Letter of Invitation

Copy this letter onto school letterhead and send it (or one like it) to the people you would like to have as committee members.

---

Dear

In your response to our recent school survey, you indicated an interest in several areas, leading us to believe that you might want to serve on our school's Grant Committee. This committee will be formulating long range plans to make our school a better place by applying for grants which are available to schools, and we would like to invite you to be part of this undertaking.

To begin with, we will all be writing broad goal statements. Later, we will ask individuals and groups within the committee to do research, gather data, and identify specific needs in our school.

A tentative schedule is enclosed with this letter. Only the first meeting has been assigned a date because we want to poll the group and determine the best meeting time for everyone.

Thank you for your interest and your time. We hope to see you at the first meeting.

Sincerely,

# How to Start Planning

## Building a Team *(cont.)*

Here is an example of how to fill out page 42. Include a copy of your schedule with each of your invitation letters.

## Grant Committee Schedule—Example

| Date | Meeting | Meeting Place | Time |
|------|---------|---------------|------|
| 10-23 | First Meeting<br><br>*Organizational/Setting Schedule/Getting Acquainted* | *teachers' lounge* | *4:30 p.m.* |
| | Second Meeting<br><br>*Discussion of Survey Results* | | |
| | Third Meeting<br><br>*Goal Statements* | | |
| | *What Is a Goal?* | | |
| | *How to Write Goal Statements* | | |
| | Fourth Meeting<br><br>*Goal Writing Workshop* | | |
| | Fifth Meeting<br><br>*Subject to Be Determined* | | |

# How to Start Planning

## Building a Team *(cont.)*

Fill out this schedule and enclose copies of it with your invitation letters.

## Grant Committee Schedule

| Date | Meeting | Meeting Place | Time |
|------|---------|---------------|------|
|  | First Meeting |  |  |
|  | Second Meeting |  |  |
|  | Third Meeting |  |  |
|  | Fourth Meeting |  |  |
|  | Fifth Meeting |  |  |

## Letter of Appreciation

Copy this letter on school letterhead and send it (or one like it) to the people who attended your first committee meeting.

------------------------------------------------------------------------

Dear

Thank you for attending the first meeting of our newly formed Grant Committee. Your interest in our school and your willingness to commit time and energy to this project are deeply appreciated. Our initial discussion indicates that we can look forward to a productive experience for everyone involved.

Although we are looking ahead to the grants we will write and have funded, your interest alone during this preliminary period will improve our school because of the effect it will have on school morale and optimism.

The teachers appreciate your interest and the students will certainly benefit from the work of this committee as it goes into action.

We are looking forward to seeing you at the next meeting.

Sincerely,

_____

# How to Start Planning

## Building a Team (cont.)

Use this form at your Goal Writing Workshop to get people started.

## Goal Writing Workshop

### Goals Are Broad Statements

Goals are broad sweeping statements written in general terms. (See the definition of goal/vision/mission statement on page 89.) They deal with program outcomes and are not measurable. They should reflect the views of the school community.

### Look at Your Survey Tabulations

✐ If a large group of parents responding to your survey wanted their children to be exposed to great art throughout history, you might write a goal statement like this:

The goal of **Project AH-HA** (Art in History, History in Art) is to enhance instruction in history with works of art that help students understand and remember stories linking other times and cultures with their own.

✐ If the students in your school are enjoying the geography program that is already being offered and parents would like to see the program expanded, you might write a goal statement like this:

The goal of **Project GIFT** (Geography Instruction For Teachers) is to offer teachers the opportunity to learn about the new National Geography Standards.

✐ If the parents who responded to your survey put new computer software high on their list of new material they want for the school, an appropriate goal statement might be:

The goal of **Project Software** is to provide a variety of up-to-date software for the existing computer lab and in-service instructions on their uses.

# How to Start Planning

## Building a Team *(cont.)*

### Goal Writing Workshop

Use this form to get started at your Goal Writing Workshop. Select some of the priorities from the school survey and write them below. Then try writing your own goal statements to go with them. (You do not have to think up clever project names, but sometimes this can be fun.)

1. Priority statement from survey: _____

   _____

   _____

   Matching goal statement: _____

   _____

   _____

2. Priority statement from survey: _____

   _____

   _____

   Matching goal statement: _____

   _____

   _____

3. Priority statement from survey: _____

   _____

   _____

   Matching goal statement: _____

   _____

   _____

# How to Start Planning

## Building a Team (cont.)

This is an example of how the committee's researchers might use the form on page 47 to keep track of what they learn.

## Research Record—Example

**Title of Book or Article:** _Grantseeking Primer for Classroom Leaders_

**Author:** _David G. Bauer_

**Publishing Information:** _Scholastic 1994_

**Summary:** _An overall look at the grant process. Covers everything from "why" to "how."_

_Very high level._

**Unique Quality:** _Embodies the personal experience of the author._

**Other Books/Articles by the Author:** _____

**Name of Researcher:** _Nick Baker_

# How to Start Planning

## Building a Team *(cont.)*

Give this form or something similar to the committee's researchers to use for keeping track of what they learn.

## Research Record—Form

**Title of Book or Article:** _____

_____

**Author:** _____

**Publishing Information:** _____

_____

**Summary:** _____

_____

_____

_____

_____

**Unique Quality:** _____

_____

_____

_____

**Other Books/Articles by the Author:** _____

_____

_____

**Name of Researcher:** _____

# How to Start Planning

## Building a Team *(cont.)*

This is an example of how the form on page 49 could be used by the committee's liaison people to keep track of the contacts they make.

---

### Networking Record—Example

**Date:** _11/30_

**Name of Contact:** _Nancy Blair_

**Address:** _N/A_

**Phone Number:** _(213) 555-8000 ext. 714_

**Organization:** _Junior Chamber of Commerce_

**Interest Expressed:** _Would like to help with the publicity for community coverage at the next major school event._

**Liaison Person:** _Lisa Smythe_

---

# How to Start Planning

## Building a Team (cont.)

### Networking Record—Form

Give this form or a similar one to the committee's liaisons to keep track of the contacts they make.

---

**Networking Record—Example**

Date: _____

Name of Contact: _____

Address: _____

_____

Phone Number: _____

Organization: _____

Interest Expressed: _____

_____

_____

_____

_____

_____

_____

_____

_____

_____

Liaison Person: _____

---

# How to Start Planning

## Identifying Needs

### Needs in the Planning Stage

The identification of needs in the planning stage of grant writing is a much less specific process than it will be later on when you will be writing a needs statement for a particular grant proposal. At this stage you will be identifying the areas of need and collecting the statistics to support your position.

### Needs for Problems

Your needs are actually the problems you see in your school. They are the description of the conditions as they exist right now.

### Needs Are Inextricably Connected to Solutions

At the planning stage you will identify many problems. Some you will never present in a grant proposal simply because you cannot solve them. (For example, if the basic problem you see in your school is poverty, unless you can solve the problem, you will not want to establish it as a need in a proposal.)

### A Pool of Needs

Certainly, you will identify more needs than you could ever present in just one proposal. You will be identifying a *pool* of needs that you can dip into as required. Also, you will be collecting the data to support your position.

### Backing up Your Needs with Facts

It is not enough to state your needs; you will be expected to prove them. Have your statisticians start to collect data and inventory materials and supplies. Give them a file cabinet and roomy folders. They might be labeled in the following way and contain these listed materials and other pieces of information.

#### *Areas of the Curriculum*

*Reading*

❖ test scores (state, district, school, classroom)

❖ list of available materials by school, grade level, and classroom (basal readers, literature sets, phonics materials, library collections, videos)

# How to Start Planning

## Identifying Needs *(cont.)*

---

### *Areas of the Curriculum* *(cont.)*

**Writing**

❖ test scores (state, district, school, classroom)

❖ list of available materials by school, grade level, and classroom (language/grammar books, portfolios, computers with word processing capability)

**Math**

❖ test scores (state, district, school, classroom)

❖ lists of available materials by school, grade level, and classroom (math books; sets of manipulatives; videos; miscellaneous supplies such as measuring devices, compasses and protractors, etc.)

**Science**

❖ test scores (state, district, school, classroom)

❖ lists of available materials by school, grade level, and classroom (science books; videos; equipment such as science kits, microscopes, and general supplies for performing experiments and investigations)

**Social Studies**

❖ test scores (state, district, school, classroom)

❖ list of available materials by school, grade level, and classroom (history books, geography books, wall maps, globes, reference materials, related literature)

**Physical Education**

❖ test scores (national, state, district, school, classroom)

❖ lists of available materials by school, grade level, and classroom (playground and sports equipment such as slides, swings, climbing apparatuses, balls, bats, bases, backstops, tetherballs, volleyball courts and nets, etc.)

**Art**

❖ lists of available materials by school, grade level, and classroom (paper, crayons, paints, brushes, markers, etc.)

**Music**

❖ lists of available materials by school, grade level, and classroom (music books, recordings, instruments, etc.)

---

# How to Start Planning

## Identifying Needs *(cont.)*

### *Other Areas*

***Elementary School Programs***
- ❖ district and state review data

***High School Programs***
- ❖ SAT scores/district and state review data

***Non-English Speaking Students***
- ❖ (changing) demographics

***Racial/Ethnic Tensions***
- ❖ (changing) demographics

***Tardiness/Truancy***
- ❖ school attendance records

***Behavior Problems***
- ❖ suspensions/expulsions

***Lack of Equipment and Materials***
- ❖ lists as compared to student population

***Hunger***
- ❖ number of students receiving free meals

## Ready for Anything

With this kind of data, amassed and categorized, you will be ready to describe and prove your needs for any grant that comes along. You will also have a better picture of what you are dealing with on a day to day basis in your school. Just the identification of a problem area often suggests a common sense solution that does not demand grant money at all, or perhaps suggests a way to get started while you are waiting, thereby putting yourself in a better position to have your grant funded when you apply.

# How to Start Planning

## Identifying Needs *(cont.)*

Use this form to summarize the various test scores at the classroom, school, district, and state levels. Record each curriculum area on a separate copy of this page.

---

## Collection of Test Scores

**Year** _____

**Curriculum Area**

_____

**State Tests and Scores:**

**District Tests and Scores:**

**School Tests and Scores:**

---

# How to Start Planning

## Identifying Needs *(cont.)*

---

## Reading Materials Inventory

Year _____

Grade Level _____

Classroom _____

### Basal Readers

Name: _____   Quantity: _____

Name: _____   Quantity: _____

Name: _____   Quantity: _____

### Literature Sets

Name: _____   Quantity: _____

Name: _____   Quantity: _____

Name: _____   Quantity: _____

### Phonics Materials

Name: _____   Quantity: _____

Name: _____   Quantity: _____

Name: _____   Quantity: _____

### Library Collections

Grade Level Spread: _____

Number of Volumes: _____

### Videos

Subjects: _____

_____

_____

Number of Tapes: _____

---

# How to Start Planning

## Identifying Needs *(cont.)*

## Reading Materials Inventory

Year _____

Grade Level _____

Classroom _____

### Language/Grammar Books

    Name: _____      Quantity: _____

    Name: _____      Quantity: _____

    Name: _____      Quantity: _____

### Portfolios in the Classroom

    Collection Portfolios: _____

    Showcase Portfolios: _____

### Computer Access

_____

_____

### Word Processing Program

_____

_____

### Other Materials

_____

_____

# How to Start Planning

## Identifying Needs *(cont.)*

## Math Materials Inventory

Year _____

Grade Level _____

Classroom _____

### Math Books

    Name: _____     Quantity: _____

    Name: _____     Quantity: _____

    Name: _____     Quantity: _____

### Sets of Manipulatives

    Name: _____     Quantity: _____

    Name: _____     Quantity: _____

    Name: _____     Quantity: _____

### Miscellaneous Supplies

    Name: _____     Quantity: _____

    Name: _____     Quantity: _____

    Name: _____     Quantity: _____

### Videos

    Subjects: _____

    _____

    _____

    Number of Tapes: _____

## Science Materials Inventory

Year _____

Grade Level_____

Classroom _____

### Science Books

Name: _____ Quantity: _____

Name: _____ Quantity: _____

Name: _____ Quantity: _____

### Videos

Subjects: _____

Number of Tapes: _____

### Science Kits

Name: _____

Name: _____

Name: _____

Name: _____

### Microscopes and Other Equipment

Name: _____ Quantity: _____

Name: _____ Quantity: _____

Name: _____ Quantity: _____

## Social Studies Materials Inventory

Year _____

Grade Level_____

Classroom _____

### History Books

Name: _____ Quantity: _____

Name: _____ Quantity: _____

Name: _____ Quantity: _____

### Geography Books

Name: _____ Quantity: _____

Name: _____ Quantity: _____

Name: _____ Quantity: _____

### Related Literature

Name: _____ Quantity: _____

Name: _____ Quantity: _____

Name: _____ Quantity: _____

### Reference Materials

### Wall Maps

Name:_____

Name:_____

Name:_____

### Globes

Quantity: _____

# How to Start Planning

## Identifying Needs *(cont.)*

---

## Physical Education Materials Inventory

Year _____

Grade Level_____

**Classroom/School** *(circle one)*

### Stationary Playground Equipment

Slides:_____

Swings: _____

Climbing Apparatus:_____

Basketball Courts: _____

Volleyball Courts:_____

### Sports Equipment

Balls (footballs, baseballs, basketballs, volleyballs, soccerballs, all-purpose playground balls):

_____

_____

_____

Bases:_____

Portable Backstops: _____

Tetherballs: _____

Nets: _____

Other:_____

_____

---

# How to Start Planning

## Identifying Needs *(cont.)*

---

### Art Materials Inventory

**Note:** Be sure to differentiate between the materials supplied by the school and those purchased or collected by teacher.

Year _____

Grade Level _____

Classroom _____

**Paper**

     Kind: _____      Quantity: _____

     Kind: _____      Quantity: _____

     Kind: _____      Quantity: _____

**Paint**

     Kind: _____      Quantity: _____

     Kind: _____      Quantity: _____

     Kind: _____      Quantity: _____

**Crayons/Colored Pencils/Markers**

     Kind: _____      Quantity: _____

     Kind: _____      Quantity: _____

     Kind: _____      Quantity: _____

**Miscellaneous Materials**

_____

_____

# How to Start Planning

## Identifying Needs *(cont.)*

## Music Materials Inventory

Year _____

Grade Level _____

Classroom _____

### Music Books

Name: _____ Quantity: _____

Name: _____ Quantity: _____

Name: _____ Quantity: _____

### Recordings

Records: _____ Quantity: _____

Tapes: _____ Quantity: _____

Compact Disks: _____ Quantity: _____

### Players

Record: _____ Quantity: _____

Tapes: _____ Quantity: _____

Compact Disk: _____ Quantity: _____

### Instruments

Name: _____ Quantity: _____

Name: _____ Quantity: _____

Name: _____ Quantity: _____

### Other _____

# How to Start Planning

## Identifying Needs *(cont.)*

---

### Technology Inventory

Year _____

Grade Level_____

Classroom/School *(circle one)*

| | Yes *(How many?)* | No | Used by How Many Students? |
|---|---|---|---|
| **TV Sets** | | | |
| **VCRs** | | | |
| **Computers** (list make and model) | | | |
| | | | |
| | | | |
| | | | |
| **Printers** (list make and model) | | | |
| | | | |
| | | | |
| | | | |
| **Modems** | | | |
| **On-Line Access** | | | |

**Note:** You may wish to tally any other forms of technology on the back of this page (i.e. laserdisc players, CD ROM drives, overhead projectors).

---

# How to Start Planning

## Identifying Needs *(cont.)*

---

## School Profile

Use this form to produce a school profile.

### A. Demographics and Special Programs

1. Grade levels at the school (circle all that apply):

   K  1  2  3  4  5  6  7  8  9  10  11  12  Adult

2. Special programs at the school site (circle all that apply):

   a. Special Education            e. Visual and Performing Arts
   b. Bilingual/ESL/Migrant Ed.    f. GATE
   c. Foreign Language             g. Other (specify): _____
   d. Vocational                   _____

### B. School-Based Programs *(circle "E" for existing, "P" for planned, "N" for none):*

| | | | |
|---|---|---|---|
| 1. School Improvement | E | P | N |
| 2. Chapter 1 | E | P | N |
| 3. Chapter 2 | E | P | N |
| 4. SB 1882 (high schools only) | E | P | N |
| 5. Coor. School-Based Program (AB 777) | E | P | N |
| 6. SB 1274 "Planning to Plan" (restructuring) | E | P | N |
| 7. District initiated school-based management | E | P | N |
| 8. AB 40 Alternative Assessment | E | P | N |
| 9. Other (specify): _____ | E | P | N |

### C. School-Based Planning Committees *(circle "E" for existing, "P" for planned, "N" for none):*

| | | | |
|---|---|---|---|
| 1. School Site Council | E | P | N |
| 2. Chapter 1 Committee | E | P | N |
| 3. Other (specify): _____ | E | P | N |

### D. Curriculum Area(s) Needing Improvement *(circle "M" for major improvement, "S" for some improvement, "N" for improvement not needed):*

| | | | |
|---|---|---|---|
| 1. English-Language Arts | M | S | N |
| 2. Mathematics | M | S | N |
| 3. Science | M | S | N |
| 4. History-Social Science | M | S | N |
| 5. Foreign Language | M | S | N |
| 6. Vocational | M | S | N |
| 7. Visual and Performing Arts | M | S | N |
| 8. Health Education | M | S | N |
| 9. Physical Education | M | S | N |
| 10. Other (specify): _____ | M | S | N |

# How to Start Planning

## Identifying Solutions

### Solutions in the Planning Stage

The identification of solutions in the planning stage of grant writing lies about halfway between the needs or problems you have identified and the objectives you will be writing for an actual grant proposal. Your planning solutions can still be qualitative but your objectives must be quantitative, that is written in terms of a measurable student outcome.

### Solutions Are Objectives

The solutions that you are going to create to solve the problems you have identified (the *is*) can be thought of as the *should*. They are the descriptions of what things will look like when the problems have been fixed.

### Solutions Are Inextricably Connected to Needs

Just as you would not want to propose a problem to which there is no solution, you will not create a solution that does not answer an identified need. (If, for example, all of your students are incredibly well-behaved, you will not want to create a program for behavior modification!) However, you should not be in a position where you have not only identified, but also prioritized, a good number of real needs by means of your school survey. You have amassed an enormous amount of hard data that can be used to support those needs. Now comes the easy part—you are going to devise solutions. And then comes the hard part—you are going to practice stating them as measurable learner outcomes. But do not give up because then comes the creative part—you will get to plan the activities.

### Confusing Terminology

Sometimes the terminology is so confusing that it masks the concepts. Perhaps you have been thinking all along, "But when are we going to say what we are actually going to do?" Not yet. First, you must identify the problem (need). Then, you will tell how you will know when the solution (objective) has been accomplished. Finally, you will go back and construct the methods (activities) that will move you from one to the other.

Of course, you have probably had a tentative plan for getting from one place to another all along, and that is good. It all has to fit together like a giant puzzle in the end anyway, and knowing how you want to accomplish your objective will keep you focused.

### The Objective

The objective, or measurable learner outcome, must describe the solution as it relates to the need, identify who will be affected, give a time frame, and tell how you will know when your objective has been reached, using hard data if possible.

# How to Start Planning

## Identifying Solutions *(cont.)*

There is often a noticeable difference between what is in our schools and what should be. Look at the sample below. Then, practice writing your own *should* statements.

## The Is/Should Model

| What Is | What Should Be | |
|---|---|---|
| **Identified Need** | **Qualitative Solution** | **Measurable Objective** |
| About 90% of the fourth grade students are reading below grade level as measured by the district reading test. | Fourth grade students will improve their reading skills. | By June, 1999, 100% of fourth grade students will read at or above grade level as measured by the district reading test. |
| Only five third grade students per day can use computers because of scheduling problems. | | |
| Sixth grade students must share geography books and cannot take them home for homework on a daily basis. | | |

# How to Start Planning

## Identifying Solutions *(cont.)*

Now try the same exercise using some of your own identified needs.

## The Is/Should Model

| What Is | What Should Be | |
|---|---|---|
| **Identified Need** | **Qualitative Solution** | **Measurable Objective** |
| | | |
| | | |
| | | |

# How to Start Planning

## Identifying Solutions *(cont.)*

Look at the model below and then brainstorm the methods (activities) you could use to achieve your objective.

## The Activities

| What Is | What Should Be | |
|---|---|---|
| **Identified Need** | **Qualitative Solution** | **Measurable Objective** |
| About 90% of fourth grade students are reading below grade level as measured by the district reading test. | Fourth grade students will improve their reading skills. | By June, 1999, 100% of fourth grade students will read at or above grade level as measured by the district reading test. |

### Methods/Activities

## The Activities *(cont.)*

Insert one of your own statements below. Then, brainstorm the methods (activities) you could use to achieve your objective.

| What Is | What Should Be | |
|---|---|---|
| **Identified Need** | **Qualitative Solution** | **Measurable Objective** |
| | | |

**Methods/Activities**

# How to Start Planning

## Identifying Funding Sources

### Now That We Have Done All This Planning . . .

Actually identifying a funding source is different from learning about funding sources. If you have visited one of the Foundation Centers (pages 11–22), read all of the articles, and subscribed to all of the newsletters (page 240), it is now time to really get to work writing letters and calling people.

It is also time to think about alternative funding sources. If your parent organization has had a fundraiser and wants to give you the proceeds, or the graduating students want to leave a gift to the school, or a local company is upgrading and wants to give you all of its old computers and printers, thank them and take whatever they have to offer. Money is money, technology is technology, and it is easier to write a thank-you note than a grant proposal!

### Set a Goal

However, back to reality. Divide up a possible list of grant sources in some fair way and send your committee members off to dig up grants. Give them the Contact Form on page 70. (Award prizes at your next meeting to the person who finds the most grants and the person who finds the most generous grant.)

### Lay the Grants on the Table

By now, all of you will be familiar with the *is* in your school, so lay the grants on the table, pass them around, and read them. (Number the grants and use the Grant Comparison Form on page 71 to keep track.) *This one* will demand a population different from the one you have; *that one*, the big one, will demand more matching funds than you feel you can raise on your first try; *but here is one that just might work for you.*

### The Ah-Ha Moment

When you find a grant that fits your needs, take a minute or two to congratulate yourselves, but not too long because now it is time to start writing.

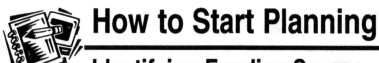

# How to Start Planning

## Identifying Funding Sources *(cont.)*

Make multiple copies of this form and pass them out to the committee members.

---

### Contact Form

Funder: _____

Telephone #: _____

FAX #: _____

Contact: _____

Address: _____

Result: _____

---

### Contact Form

Funder: _____

Telephone #: _____

FAX #: _____

Contact: _____

Address: _____

Result: _____

---

# How to Start Planning

## Identifying Funding Sources *(cont.)*

Use this form to keep track of the grants you are comparing. First, randomly number the grants and then mark the characteristics you notice about each one on the chart below.

### Grant Comparison Chart

|                          | 1 | 2 | 3 | 4 | 5 | 6 | 7 | 8 | 9 | 10 | 11 | 12 |
|--------------------------|---|---|---|---|---|---|---|---|---|----|----|----|
| Classroom                |   |   |   |   |   |   |   |   |   |    |    |    |
| Team                     |   |   |   |   |   |   |   |   |   |    |    |    |
| Whole School             |   |   |   |   |   |   |   |   |   |    |    |    |
| District                 |   |   |   |   |   |   |   |   |   |    |    |    |
| Partnership              |   |   |   |   |   |   |   |   |   |    |    |    |
| Matching Funds           |   |   |   |   |   |   |   |   |   |    |    |    |
| Specific Population       |   |   |   |   |   |   |   |   |   |    |    |    |
| Technology               |   |   |   |   |   |   |   |   |   |    |    |    |
| Language Arts            |   |   |   |   |   |   |   |   |   |    |    |    |
| Math                     |   |   |   |   |   |   |   |   |   |    |    |    |
| Science                  |   |   |   |   |   |   |   |   |   |    |    |    |
| Social Studies           |   |   |   |   |   |   |   |   |   |    |    |    |
| Due Date                 |   |   |   |   |   |   |   |   |   |    |    |    |

# Grants for Schools—Part Two

## Table of Contents

# How to Start Writing

## The Real Thing

### Of Course You Can Write It

Stage fright is normal at this point. In spite of the fact that you just finished comparing grants and noting their differences, you probably observed that they all have one thing in common. They are intimidating. But familiarity will breed confidence, in this case, and you will soon think nothing of composing a table of contents or dashing off an abstract.

### Follow Directions

The most important thing to do is follow directions. The directions for most grant proposals are very specific.

They say big things like this:

> A project will not be considered eligible for funding unless the applicant documents the capacity to supply matching funds. Applications that do not meet this requirement will be rejected.

And little things like this:

> Use a 12 pt. font with no more than six lines to an inch. Read all the directions and follow them exactly.

### Use Your Critics

Strive for clarity in your writing. The critical people you asked to be on the Grant Committee back in the planning phase will become invaluable now. Have them read everything. If something is not clear to even one of them, change it and make it clear.

Have some people who are not on the committee read the proposal too. Even your critics may miss things because they have become invested in the whole process. See if someone who was not involved in the planning, understands what you are saying.

### Grammar and Spelling Are Important

Use a good spelling check program and find someone with a knack for grammar to edit your work. Watch your homonyms because the spelling check program will not pick them up and double-check your use of apostrophes in possessives. Do not use contractions at all. (See The Mechanics of Writing on pages 75–77.)

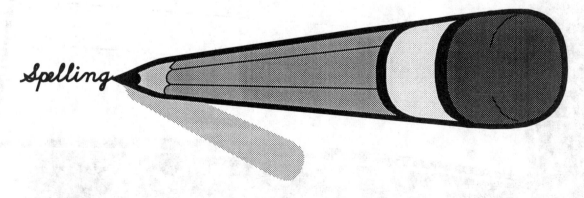

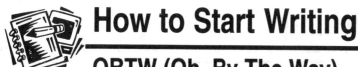

# How to Start Writing

## OBTW (Oh, By The Way)

### Keep a Hard Copy of Everything as You Go Along

This is not the time to save on paper. If you make a change, rerun the page immediately and throw away the old page.

Take reasonable precautions about sharing disks and copying to and from your hard drive. It is easy to write over new material with outdated material if more than one person is writing. However, if you have hard copy, the worst that can happen is that you may need to reenter something.

### Number Your Pages, If Required or Allowed

If you are not sure about the numbering procedure, call the funder and enquire. In the meantime, at least number the pages of your own copy lightly in pencil. Take the time to erase and renumber everything if you insert a page somewhere. There is nothing more frustrating than trying to put the pages back in order, if you drop them and they scatter. If you drop the unnumbered "good" copy, you can put the pages back in order according to the copy that is numbered in pencil.

On the software you are using, learn how to make headers, footers, and how to number the pages sequentially before you start to write. Also, learn how to suppress the numbering as required. (Inserting this information at the last minute will move everything around on your pages and you do not want to be doing this the night before your proposal must be in the mail.)

### When in Doubt, Call the Funder

If you need more information about anything, call the funder of the grant for clarification. This suggestion will be repeated throughout the book. When you come across the funder's information numbers, write them here. Also, note the mailing address.

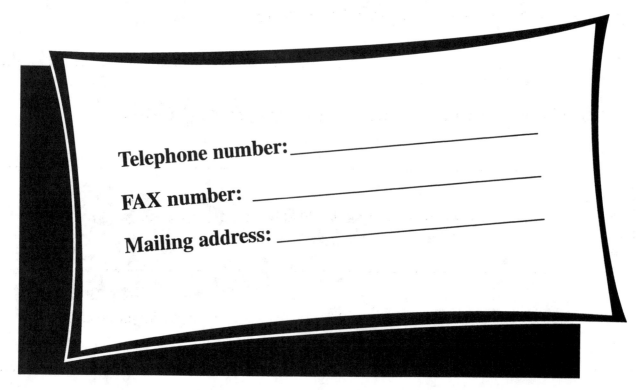

Telephone number: _____

FAX number: _____

Mailing address: _____

# How to Start Writing

## The Mechanics of Writing

Take the time to brush up on your technical writing skills by finding the errors in these sentences and then writing them correctly.

1. Each individual student will be responsible for their own portfolio.

   _____

2. The scope of these two projects are very broad.

   _____

3. Our principle helped from the committee and attends every meeting.

   _____

4. They're will be at least five teachers in there area to make sure their well-behaved.

   _____

5. The childrens' work will be displayed in the library.

   _____

6. All studnets will be involved both in the process and in it's evaluation.

   _____

7. All students will be evaluated appropriately at his or her own level.

   _____

8. Simply because we want to make school as enjoyable as possible for children.

   _____

# How to Start Writing

## The Mechanics of Writing *(cont.)*

Here are the answers to page 75, including explanations.

1. Each individual student will be responsible for their own portfolio.

   *Each individual student will be responsible for his or her own portfolio.*

   ❏ Student is singular so the pronoun(s) that refer to it must be singular too. The rule is "Pronouns must agree with their antecedents in number."

2. The scope of these two projects are very broad.

   *The scope of these two projects is very broad.*

   ❏ The subject of this sentence is scope, a singular noun which takes a singular verb, is. The rule is "Nouns or pronouns which come between the subject and the verb do not affect the number of the verb."

3. Our principle helped from the committee and attends every meeting.

   ❏ *Our principal helped form the committee and attends every meeting.*

   ❏ Principle means a rule of conduct; principal means chief or head, such as the head of a school.

   ❏ From is a common typing error for form; unfortunately, the spelling programs will not pick it up because it is a correctly spelled word.

4. They're will be at least five teachers in there area to make sure their well-behaved.

   *There will be at least five teachers in their area to make sure they're well-behaved.*

   ❏ They're means "They are." There means "in that place." Their is possessive and it means "belonging to them."

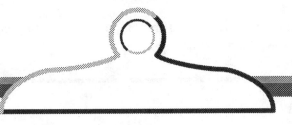

5. The childrens' work will be displayed in the library.

   *The children's work will be displayed in the library.*

   ❑ Children is already a plural noun so the apostrophe comes before the s.

6. All studnets will be involved both in the process and in it's evaluation.

   *All students will be involved both in the process and in its evaluation.*

   ❑ Studnets is probably the number one typographical error. The spelling programs will catch it but it is easy to miss it when you just look over a page.

   ❑ The contraction it's means "it is." The possessive form is its with no apostrophe.

7. All students will be evaluated appropriately at his or her own level.

   *All students will be evaluated appropriately at their own levels.*

   ❑ Students is a plural noun so the pronoun that refers to it must be plural too. The rule is "Pronouns must agree with their antecedents in number."

   ❑ Level becomes levels to agree in number also.

8. Simply because we want to make school as enjoyable as possible for children.

   *We are proposing this simply because we want to make school as enjoyable as possible for children.*

   ❑ The sentence, as originally written, is a fragment.

# How to Start Writing

## Grant Elements—Outline

Use the outline below and the definitions starting on page 81 to complete your Writing Checklist (pages 79 and 80) for each grant for which you are applying.

## Outline

### I. Formatting Issues

  A. Determine the exact number of pages you must have or are allowed to have. Check the following items:

    1. Minimum number required (if there is one)

    2. Maximum number allowed

    3. Whether or not attachments are allowed

  B. Check the page layout requirements.

    1. Width of margins

    2. Size of font

    3. Justification

    4. Spacing of lines

    5. Numbering of pages

### II. Required and/or Allowed Elements Which May Include:

  A. Title

  B. Abstract

  C. Table of Contents

  D. Introduction

  E. Goal/Vision/Mission Statement

  F. Statement of Needs

  G. Objectives (stated in measurable terms)

  H. Activities (how objective will be met)

  I. Management

  J. Personnel

  K. Time Lines

  L. Resources (as solutions)

  M. Evaluation

  N. Dissemination

  O. Budget

  P. Attachments

# How to Start Writing

## Grant Elements —Writing Checklist

Make photocopies of pages 74, 78-80, and the definition pages starting on page 81 and give a set to everyone involved in preparing your grant proposal. Ask all of the participants to be on the lookout for discrepancies from the criteria you have listed. (It is easy to set the margins incorrectly or slip into the wrong type size when you are concentrating on your ideas and how to best express them.)

Check and double check all of the formatting issues before you start to write anything. It is hard to cut your pages after you have labored over the perfect wording. On most grant proposals, you are not allowed to shrink your text to fit on a page. If the readers (scorers, judges) see that you did not follow the formatting requirements, they may be bound by the rules to throw out your proposal without reading it.

---

### Formatting Issues

**A. Number of Pages**

1. Minimum number required _____

2. Maximum number allowed _____

3. Attachments allowed (check one)  ❏ Yes  ❏ No

**B. Layout of Pages**

1. Width of margins_____

2. Size of font _____

3. Justification _____

4. Spacing of lines_____

5. Numbering of lines _____

---

# How to Start Writing

## Grant Elements—Writing Checklist *(cont.)*

Read and reread the definitions of these elements. If an element is called something else in your grant, note the term under the column entitled AKA (Also Known As).

| Elements | Required | Allowed | AKA |
|---|---|---|---|
| Title | | | |
| Abstract | | | |
| Table of Contents | | | |
| Introduction | | | |
| Goal/Vision/Mission | | | |
| Statement of Needs | | | |
| Objectives | | | |
| Activities | | | |
| Management | | | |
| Personnel | | | |
| Time Lines | | | |
| Resources | | | |
| Evaluation | | | |
| Dissemination | | | |
| Budget | | | |
| Attachments | | | |
| (If attachments are allowed, what will they consist of? Is there anything that you *cannot* attach?) _____ | | | |

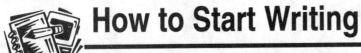

# How to Start Writing

## Grant Elements—Definitions

(If you need more information about how any of the formatting issues or grant proposal elements discussed below apply to your specific proposal, call the funder of the grant for clarification. Remember, the various elements may be given different names and occur in different orders.)

### Formatting Issues

Formatting issues include all of the technical criteria for putting your words on paper. Your grant proposal can be thrown out without being read, if you do not follow the stated criteria asked for in the particular grant proposal you are writing.

All of the technical requirements for grant writing are extremely important. Comb the document for instructions about the number of pages (minimum and maximum), the number of lines per page, the spacing of the lines, the size of all margins, the type of justification, the numbering of the pages, and the size of the type font or number of characters per inch. Do not shrink anything to fit the page unless you are sure that this is allowed.

---

## Summary

1. **Number of pages**

   • Count them.

2. **Number of lines per page**

   • Count them.

3. **Spacing of lines**

   • Spacing is usually single or double. Do not use 1.5 spacing.

4. **Size of margins**

   • Set them and then measure them on the page.

5. **Justification**

   • Some grants permit full justification; others want left justification with the right side left "ragged."

6. **Type size**

   • Set the type size and then measure the characters on the page.

---

## Grant Elements Definitions *(cont.)*

The definitions on this and the following pages are elements which may be included in a grant proposal.

### Title

While some experts do not even mention the title of the project as a grant element, others feel that it is of the utmost importance because it identifies the proposal in the minds of the readers (judges, graders) and makes it distinctive in their memories. It is important, however, not to get too "cutesy" or to create an unmanageable acronym. If you do create an acronym, define it every time it is used—for example, Project GIFT (Geography Instruction For Teachers).

Experts who think titles are important also recommend using boldface type, underlining, or quotation marks to call attention to the title each time it occurs in the text. (See pages 44–45, Goal Writing Workshop.)

### Abstract

The abstract, sometimes called the overview or the summary, is a statement which gives a synopsis of your whole grant proposal. Each section of the proposal should be represented in the abstract. In it you should identify yourself, support your credibility, present your reason for applying (need), state your objectives, mention the activities you will undertake, and give the total amount the project will cost.

An abstract is required for federal grants and some others as well. It is a good idea to include an abstract even if it is not required, but only if it does not cause you to exceed the maximum number of pages you can have.

Some grant writers advise writing the abstract first in order to focus and define your project, but most experts recommend writing it last in order to make it reflect a true picture of your proposal. If you do write it first, remember to revise it if necessary to encompass any changes you may have made in the process of writing.

An abstract, if it is included, almost always (there are exceptions to every rule) appears as the first page of the grant proposal. It should not be longer than one page and is usually much shorter. Some grant proposals give you a space on the cover sheet for the summary (abstract). Since it is right there in front, it will certainly be the first thing to be read.

Sometimes the abstract is used as a screening mechanism so it might be the only thing read, unless it catches the interest of the person doing the screening. Even if the reader goes on to peruse your proposal to the very end, a clear abstract will have given enough information about what you are hoping to do to serve as a reference point for everything that follows.

# How to Start Writing

## Grant Elements—Definitions *(cont.)*

**Title Activity:** Think up some appropriate and clever names for these proposals. Create an acronym if possible.

1. a proposal to obtain funds for playground equipment in a kindergarten

   _____

2. a proposal to fund a computer lab in a middle school

   _____

3. a proposal to acquire math manipulatives in the primary grades

   _____

4. a proposal to buy science kits for an established science lab in the upper elementary grades

   _____

5. a proposal to obtain funds for costumes for a touring high school drama department

   _____

6. a proposal to obtain funds for a variety of field trips in the elementary school

   _____

7. a proposal that would benefit Limited English Proficiency (LEP) students

   _____

8. a proposal to fund a free breakfast program for needy students

   _____

# How to Start Writing

## Grant Elements—Definitions *(cont.)*

**Abstract Activity:** Read this abstract (a very short one from a proposal written by one teacher for a classroom grant) in the light of what you have just learned about writing one.

### Program Summary

*Project Picture This* will provide my tenth grade World History students and my eleventh grade Advanced Placement students with works of art that will help them understand and remember the stories that link other times and cultures with their own. With a painting from the Louvre, for example, projected on the classroom's 25-inch (64 cm) monitor for all fifty minutes of a class period, students will not only look directly at the painting and relate it to the history under discussion, they will also perceive it peripherally. This will give them the familiarity with great works of art which promotes both historical and artistic literacy.

What is missing in the abstract?

_____

_____

_____

_____

_____

_____

Rewrite the abstract, using fictional information if necessary.

_____

_____

_____

_____

_____

_____

_____

### Abstract Check-Up:

### Program Summary

*Project Picture This* will provide my tenth grade World History students and my eleventh grade Advanced Placement students with works of art that will help them understand and remember the stories that link other times and cultures with their own. With a painting from the Louvre, for example, projected on the classroom's 25-inch (64 cm) monitor for all fifty minutes of a class period, students will not only look directly at the painting and relate it to the history under discussion, they will also perceive it peripherally. This will give them the familiarity with great works of art which promotes both historical and artistic literacy.

### Missing Information:

The applicant does not identify himself or herself. There is no attempt to establish credibility. Needs are not directly stated. There are no objectives and only the vaguest reference to an activity. The cost of the project is not mentioned. The only thing we know for sure is that they already have a 25-inch (64 cm) monitor.

### Possible Rewrite:

As a high school teacher with twelve years of experience teaching history and the humanities to advanced placement classes, I have planned a program, *Project Picture This*. This program will overcome the deficits in cultural literacy demonstrated by my classes on a teacher-constructed test drawn from the art and history sections of *The Dictionary of Cultural Literacy* by E.D. Hirsch, Jr. The Program will involve 120 students. A multi-track laser disc player will enable the students to view paintings that are relevant to and connected with their studies in history for the purpose of increasing learning retention. This learning retention will be evaluated through students' scores on Advanced Placement exams and grades on finals. The total cost of the project will be $679.00 for the disc player and a disc of art for the period under study.

# How to Start Writing

## Grant Elements—Definitions *(cont.)*

### Table of Contents

The table of contents should usually be no longer than one page, although it might be as long as two pages in some grant proposals. It should list the main sections of your proposal in the order that they are mentioned in the abstract and in which they will appear in the proposal itself. Give page numbers for each section.

The table of contents follows the abstract. It is always required in a federal grant. It can be included in other grants, but this is one of the times when you will need to check (1) the maximum number of pages allowed and (2) whether or not attachments are permitted.

See the example of a long table of contents for a federal grant on pages 87 and 88.

### Introduction

The introduction begins your narrative and sets the tone for your proposal. It often includes and overlaps with your statements of goals and needs. Depending on the length of your grant proposal, the introduction may be just the first paragraph or so of your statement of needs.

Many experts stress the idea that the introduction should not only identify the grant applicant and describe the purpose and goals of the project being proposed but it should also establish credibility. Credibility can be established in a number of ways, all of which should be used if they seem relevant. Among them are descriptions of the existing programs together with proof of achievements. This proof might consist of statistical data and statements of support. The introduction should also identify the "client base" or "target student population."

The introduction should be clear, conversational in tone, and free of educational jargon. It should tell enough about your proposal to make the reader want to know more and lead directly into the statement of needs or the problem statement.

Your introduction will obviously depend on who you are, what your goals are, and how you plan to state your problem. Double check your introduction to make sure that it includes the items listed below.

---

**Your introduction should...**

> ... identify the applicant.
>
> ... state your goals (unless there is a separate goal statement).
>
> ... mention your other successful programs and provide data and/or testimony.
>
> ... lead into your statement of needs.
>
> ... develop interest in your proposal.

---

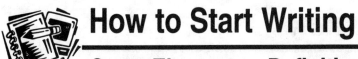

# How to Start Writing

## Grant Elements—Definitions *(cont.)*

**Table of Contents Sample:** Below is a sample table of contents for a grant for Able Project.

## Table of Contents

*©EZGrants*

# How to Start Writing

## Grant Elements—Definitions (cont.)

**Table of Contents** (cont.)

# How to Start Writing

## Grant Elements—Definitions (cont.)

### Goal/Vision/Mission Statement

Any or all of these terms can be used to refer to the broad statements of ideals that you hold for the future of education in your school or district. Unlike objectives, these statements are not measurable. They can include words such as "introduce," "provide," and "offer" since they refer to project designs rather than learner outcomes (which must be measurable). They do not provide the criteria for evaluating success. They tend to be rather lofty descriptions and should show some link to both your own educational philosophy and that of the funder.

Generally, your goal statement will be part of the introduction, but sometimes there is a special place for a separate goal statement on an application.

Check the goals you developed as part of your Goal Writing Workshop on pages 45.

Here is an example of a goal statement written to stand alone as a declaration of the far-reaching vision of the program it announces.

### The Mission Statement

> By the turn of the century, the _____ **High School Consensus Consortium** will have become an authentic and influential factor in the creation of an environment in which students understand, discuss, and respect the beliefs of each group which makes up the school population. Because of this well-developed foundation of mutual appreciation, the mediation of all differences and disputes will be the school's accepted social standard.

This is an example of a goal statement that is part of the introduction in a short grant proposal.

> **Project Poets** will provide all seventh and eighth grade language arts students with weekly sessions with a published poet provided by California Poets in the Schools, the largest writers-in-schools program in the nation.

# How to Start Writing

## Grant Elements—Definitions *(cont.)*

## Statement of Needs

This is where you explain your problem. It is the heart of your proposal. Unfortunately, the term "needs" is confusing to many writers of grant proposals. Your "need" is your *is,* the description of your current situation. It is not *what* you need. *Never* make statements such as these:

Students need to learn how to read with comprehension and pleasure.

- Teachers, as well as students, need assistance from outside experts.

- These are not statements of needs, as the term is used in grant writing.

It is probably less confusing to think of a statement of the problem instead of a statement of needs. Although some experts in this field define these terms differently, the difference is one of scope rather than basic meaning and can be disregarded except in the most sophisticated applications of the terms. You may also be asked to justify your request, give your rationale for applying, or defend your proposal. These are all different terms for this grant element.

Basically (and simply) speaking, this is where you tell what is wrong and how you know. It is the part of your proposal where you will consult and use all those folders of information and hard data you put together back in the planning stages. (See How to Start Planning: Identifying Needs on pages 50–63.)

---

**Your problem should...**

   ... correlate with your stated goals and those of the funding organization.

   ... be reasonable in its scope (potentially solvable).

   ... have statistical support (hard data).

   ... have expert support (statements and research).

   ... be stated in terms of student population (it is not your problem, per se).

   ... relate directly to the objectives that will follow (check to make sure).

---

## Statement of Needs *(cont.)*

**Sample Needs or Problem Statements:**

Here is an example of a problem statement at the elementary school level.

During the last five years, the primary students at Kennedy Elementary School have received reading instruction in a completely phonics-based program. Although students leaving third grade are excellent oral readers (able to read grade-level material at sight with 100% accuracy), they have scored poorly on tests of reading comprehension. (See Addendum II and III for a compilation and analysis of reading comprehension tests given.) We find it necessary at this time to supplement our approach to reading with a strong comprehension program. It is for this reason we are proposing **Project Read for Meaning.** Approximately 240 primary students and 180 upper elementary students would be included in this program.

Kennedy Elementary School is a medium-sized suburban school located near a large metropolitan area. In the past we have generally enjoyed a comfortable level of funding. However, recent down-sizing in the aerospace industry has had a negative impact on the whole state and our funds for new programs such as **Project Read for Meaning** are limited. Parent support for a program in reading comprehension has been difficult to motivate since their children can "read" orally with such fluency. (See Addendum III for the results of our school survey.)

Current national research supports the need for a program such as **Project Read for Meaning.** In an article in the October issue of *The Good Teacher,* Ann Authority states that comprehension is the most important indication of reading competency. *Time* magazine has featured several articles on this problem. (See Addendum IV, Articles.) Additionally, on a local level, Dr. Educator, principal of the middle school into which our school feeds, has responded to our concern about reading comprehension with a letter in support of **Project Read for Meaning.**
(See Addendum V.)

These two paragraphs are based on a needs statement taken from a project that was funded at the high school level.

According to 1993 CBEDS data, 49% of the students at East High School (a 9-12 school) belong to ethnic minorities. While this fact alone does not indicate an at-risk population, many of these students lack proficiency in English. This greatly impacts the high school curriculum and makes it extremely difficult for many of these students to perform at grade level and meet graduation requirements on time.

The Limited English Proficient (LEP) school population in our district has increased over 170% in the last five years. During the same time period, the LEP population at East High School has increased 700% from 70 students in 1988 to 494 in 1993. Current enrollment is 1,492 9th-12th graders. LEP students make up nearly one-third of our population.

# How to Start Writing

## Grant Elements—Definitions *(cont.)*

**Sample Needs or Problem Activity:** Go through your survey results of identified areas of need and find one that you feel you could describe and then support with the data you have collected. Write your statement below. If you are doing this with your Grant Committee, exchange needs statements and check for the following information:

- Does the statement draw a realistic picture of conditions as they exist?

- Does the statement give an indication of your setting and student population?

- Does the statement offer data in support of the problem(s) you are identifying?

- Does the statement offer validation of your problem?

_____

_____

_____

_____

_____

_____

_____

_____

_____

_____

_____

_____

_____

_____

_____

# How to Start Writing

## Grant Elements—Definitions *(cont.)*

Your objectives describe what the situation will look like after you have implemented your project. They are always measurable. They are written in terms of learner outcomes. They tell who will do what and when it will be done. They flow directly from the problem.

Which one of these statements is a measurable objective?

At the end of a full school year of participation in **Project Read for Meaning,** 85% of the students attending Kennedy Elementary School will score at or above grade level on the same battery of reading comprehension tests given to establish the need for this project.

**Project Read for Meaning** will dramatically improve the reading comprehension of the students attending Kennedy Elementary School.

The first statement is the measurable objective. It tells who: *85% of the students attending Kennedy Elementary School.* It tells what: *will score at or above grade level on the same battery of reading comprehension tests given to establish the need for this project.* And it tells when: *at the end of a full school year of participation in Project Read for Meaning.*

The second statement is not written in terms of learner outcome. It does not define the learner population or tell what the learner will do. The verb "improve" is not measurable. There is no time frame.

Try writing your own measurable objective for the students at Kennedy Elementary School.

_____

_____

_____

_____

_____

_____

_____

_____

_____

_____

# How to Start Writing

## Grant Elements—Definitions *(cont.)*

**Sample Objectives Activity:** Reread this statement of needs and this time write a measurable objective for it.

According to 1993 CBEDS data, 49% of the students at East High School (a 9–12 school) belong to ethnic minorities. While this fact alone does not indicate an at-risk population, many of these students lack proficiency in English. This greatly impacts the high school curriculum and makes it extremely difficult for many of these students to perform at grade level and meet graduation requirements on time.

The Limited English Proficient (LEP) school population in our district has increased over 170% in the last five years. During the same time period, the LEP population at East High School has increased 700%, from 70 students in 1988 to 494 in 1993. Current enrollment is 1,492 9th–12th graders. LEP students make up nearly one-third of our population.

_____

_____

_____

_____

_____

Now, reread your own needs statement from page 92 and write a measurable objective for it.

_____

_____

_____

_____

_____

_____

# How to Start Writing

## Grant Elements—Definitions *(cont.)*

### Activities *(How Objectives Will Be Met)*

Activities are also known as methods, methodologies, strategies, and procedures. They are the steps that will be taken to achieve the desired results, in other words, the steps that you are going to do to meet your objectives.

The activities are actually what you wanted to do in the first place, only now you know why you wanted to do them and what you will have achieved when they have been completed. Many a grant proposal has been created to make an activity financially possible or to give it some kind of official validation. This is not as unprofessional as it may seem on first reading; good teachers often make an intuitive leap from a situation as they see it from day to day to the activities they know will help the situation. (On an everyday basis, it is called writing lesson plans!) If they need money to put those activities into action, they collect the data, describe their needs, and tell how they will know when the activities have solved the problems. In other words, they write a grant proposal.

Take a few minutes to write four activities for **Project Read for Meaning.** (See page 91.)

1. _____

_____

_____

2. _____

_____

_____

3. _____

_____

_____

4. _____

_____

_____

# How to Start Writing

## Grant Elements—Definitions *(cont.)*

**Sample Activities Activity:** Now write four activities for the East High School needs and objectives developed on pages 91 and 94.

1. _____

   _____

   _____

   _____

2. _____

   _____

   _____

   _____

3. _____

   _____

   _____

   _____

4. _____

   _____

   _____

# How to Start Writing

## Grant Elements—Definitions *(cont.)*

**Sample Activities Activity** *(cont.)*

Finish up the activities section by writing four activities for your own needs and objectives developed on pages 92 and 94.

1. _____

_____

_____

_____

2. _____

_____

_____

_____

3. _____

_____

_____

_____

4. _____

_____

_____

_____

# How to Start Writing

## Grant Elements—Definitions *(cont.)*

### Management

It is important to explain how the applicant will manage the project. Who will be the project director? What will that role entail? Who will be responsible for seeing that the project proceeds as described in your proposal? This is the time for names and titles.

Since most grants do not allow funds to be spent on salaries, how will the staff be compensated? Many proposals are written to provide substitute time that frees needed staff to work on the project. All of this needs to be decided ahead of time to prevent a situation where people are expected to give more free time than is reasonable or desirable.

### Personnel

This section of the proposal should profile the important personnel connected with the project. Starting with the project director, profiles should include leadership qualifications as well as experience that is germane to the project. It should detail training that is applicable to the project as well as accounts of other successfully conducted programs. Briefer profiles of other important staff members should also be included.

### Time Lines

The time line depends upon your objectives. It should identify major bench marks and the person responsible for seeing that each one has been successfully reached. A chart is a handy device for giving a clear picture of your time line. You can construct this kind of chart by listing your activities and tests down one side and writing the months (in abbreviated form) across the top.

# How to Start Writing

## Grant Elements—Definitions *(cont.)*

**Sample Time Line Activity:** Another way to make a time line is by using a format similar to those used in organizers, listing months rather than days or weeks. Look over one of the lists of activities you compiled on page 97. Use this information to plan a time line.

   Do not forget to…

      … order materials.

      … arrange for in-service dates.

      … assign dates for pretests and posttests.

      … note the beginning and ending dates of the project.

      … note the beginning and ending dates of activities.

      … schedule field trips.

      … make your evaluation.

      … schedule project dissemination.

**Project** _____ **Time Line**

_____

**Month/Year**

_____

_____

_____

_____

**Month/Year**

_____

_____

_____

_____

**Month/Year**

_____

_____

# How to Start Writing

## Grant Elements—Definitions *(cont.)*

**Sample Time Line Activity** *(cont.)*: Make copies of this page if you need more months for your time line.

## Project _____ Time Line

_____
**Month/Year**

_____

_____

_____

_____
**Month/Year**

_____

_____

_____

_____
**Month/Year**

_____

_____

_____

_____
**Month/Year**

_____

_____

_____

# How to Start Writing

## Grant Elements—Definitions *(cont.)*

The resources section is a justification for any equipment you are requesting. If you cannot show that the item is important to the success of your project, do not include it in your proposal.

## Evaluation

The evaluation section is required by most grants. There are two kinds of evaluation. The first is the evaluation of results. (Did you meet your stated objectives?) The second is an evaluation of the process. (Did you stick to your plan?)

In order to evaluate results, you must have clearly stated them in your objectives.

- Go back and take a look at them.

- Rewrite them if necessary to make them fit what you think you will really be able to achieve. If, for example, you said that 100% of your student population would be reading at or above grade level by the end of the project, you might want to adjust the percentage.

- You may want to evaluate your progress toward these results with interim checkpoints just to make sure you are going to be where you planned to be when you planned to be there.

In order to evaluate the process, take a look at your time line.

- Is it realistic?

- Should you say you will do less in order to do it better (or at all)?

In order to make your evaluation reusable, consider how you will collect, analyze, and report the data you collect. Describe these methods and attach samples of the kinds of charts, graphs, or checklists you plan to use.

Large, complicated grants may require an outside evaluation by an expert in the field. In such cases, describe your rationale for bringing in outside evaluator(s) and describe the qualifications and credentials that make them capable of doing this job.

**Sample Evaluation Activity:** Use this form to make an evaluation of the results of the objective you wrote on page 94. Rewrite the objective if necessary.

**Objective:** _____

_____

**Evaluation Tools:**_____

_____

**Outcome:**_____

_____

_____

_____

Now, use this form to make an evaluation of the process you planned when you wrote the activities and time lines. Adjust the activities and time lines if necessary.

**Plans:** _____

_____

_____

**General Time Line:**_____

_____

_____

**Results:** _____

_____

_____

_____

**Sample Evaluation Activity** *(cont.)*: Here is another way to look at evaluation. Consider the progress of your project by filling in this chart.

| Needs | Objectives | Evaluation of Results | Process | Evaluation of Plans |
|-------|-----------|----------------------|---------|---------------------|
|       |           |                      |         |                     |

# How to Start Writing

## Grant Elements—Definitions *(cont.)*

### Dissemination

Dissemination refers to sharing the program you developed for your grant. Plans for dissemination are required in larger federal and state grants. Funders see dissemination as a way of getting more value for their investment.

Helpful dissemination plans include activities, costs, time line, and your evaluation methods, plus anything helpful you learned along the way.

Here are some ideas you might want to consider:

- Present your ideas at workshops and conferences, both locally and under the auspices of one of the educational organizations.

- Query an educational magazine or journal about submitting an article detailing your program.

- Make video tapes of your activities in action.

- Invite observers from other schools into your classroom(s).

Generate your own creative ideas:

_____

_____

_____

_____

_____

_____

_____

_____

_____

_____

_____

_____

104

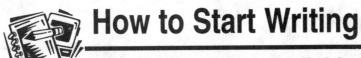

# How to Start Writing

## Grant Elements—Definitions *(cont.)*

Many people find budgets to be the scariest part of the grant writing procedure. Budgets involve a lot of research. (What is the real name of that piece of equipment I want? Who makes it? How much does it cost with taxes and shipping? How do I figure out how much it will cost next year when and if my proposal is funded? What is a purchase order anyway?)

If you did your planning well, your Grant Committee members are still meeting on a regular basis, wringing their hands, and criticizing your every move, it is true, but still they're ready to do their job. The committee's new job is to collect catalogues of equipment, software, and materials of all sorts. There are people who enjoy this process, and they are the ones who should do it.

- Somebody in the group will enjoy browsing through catalogues and writing down all of the pertinent information.

- Somebody in the group might enjoy calling sales reps from various companies and engaging in long conversations about how to extrapolate costs to make estimates for next year's prices.

- Somebody in the group might get along well with your school's office manager and can get all of the necessary information, forms, and expert help for writing purchase orders.

- Somebody may even want to write, or at least check, your budget.

The budget, of course, like everything else, is driven by the needs you identified, the objectives you wrote, and the activities you planned. If an item appears on your budget, it must be described in your narrative. If you left it out, now is the time to go back and put it in. Do not make any assumptions, and do not assume that the proposal reader will make any assumptions. If something is not described in your narrative, it cannot go into the budget.

The following are some logical steps you can take toward making your budget real and actually getting it down on paper.

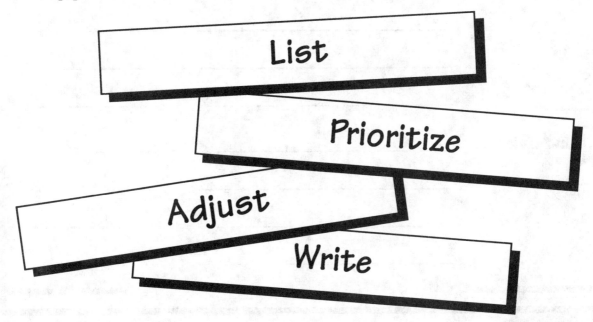

List

Prioritize

Adjust

Write

# How to Start Writing

## Grant Elements—Definitions *(cont.)*

**Sample Budget Activity:** Review what you have written so far with a fine-toothed comb and list everything that could possibly need to be paid for. Add up your total cost. If you are above the total amount available from the grant, go back and prioritize the items in each section and see where you can adjust. Be sure to make the necessary changes in your activities, if you have to eliminate something.

|  | Description | Cost |
|---|---|---|
| **Equipment:** | _____ | _____ |
|  | _____ | _____ |
|  | _____ | _____ |
|  | _____ | _____ |
| **Materials:** | _____ | _____ |
|  | _____ | _____ |
|  | _____ | _____ |
|  | _____ | _____ |
| **Supplies:** | _____ | _____ |
|  | _____ | _____ |
|  | _____ | _____ |
|  | _____ | _____ |
| **In-Services:** | _____ | _____ |
|  | _____ | _____ |
|  | _____ | _____ |
|  | _____ | _____ |

# How to Start Writing

## Grant Elements—Definitions *(cont.)*

|  | Description | Cost |
|---|---|---|
| **Substitutes:** | _____ | _____ |
|  | _____ | _____ |
|  | _____ | _____ |
| **Field Trips:** | _____ | _____ |
|  | _____ | _____ |
|  | _____ | _____ |
| **Student Awards:** | _____ | _____ |
|  | _____ | _____ |
|  | _____ | _____ |
| **Dissemination:** | _____ | _____ |
|  | _____ | _____ |
|  | _____ | _____ |
| **Fees for Services:** | _____ | _____ |
|  | _____ | _____ |
|  | _____ | _____ |
| **Miscellaneous** *(postage, photocopying, etc.):* | _____ | _____ |
|  | _____ | _____ |
|  | _____ | _____ |
|  | _____ | _____ |

# How to Start Writing

## Proposal Components Checklist

Review your proposal. Use this check-off sheet to make sure that all of the essential components have been covered.

### The Introduction . . .

_____ . . . clearly states who is applying for the funds.

_____ . . . describes the applicant and district.

_____ . . . describes the purpose and goals for the program/project.

_____ . . . describes the students/staff/administration.

_____ . . . states what accomplishments in this arena may have been accomplished.

_____ . . . leads to the assessment of the needs.

_____ . . . is short and to the point, interesting and free of "educational jargon."

### The Needs Statements . . .

_____ . . . directly relates to the district's goals, as well as the goals of the granting agency.

_____ . . . is reasonable; does not try to solve all the world's ills in one fell swoop.

_____ . . . is supported by evidence that it can work.

_____ . . . is stated in needs of the students/staff, not the person/team writing the application.

_____ . . . does not make assumptions.

_____ . . . is short and to the point, interesting and free of "educational jargon."

_____ . . . makes a compelling argument.

### The Objectives . . .

_____ . . . describes the program in measurable terms.

_____ . . . describes the student/staff that the program will benefit and how this will happen.

_____ . . . includes time lines for obtaining the objectives.

### The Activities . . .

_____ . . . describes the activities that will be used to carry out each objective.

_____ . . . relates back to each objective.

_____ . . . describes the sequence of events.

_____ . . . describes the staffing for the activity.

_____ . . . describes the students/staff involved in the activity.

_____ . . . is reasonable, and can be completed within the time lines given.

### The Evaluation . . .

_____ . . . presents the plan for measuring how the objectives are met.

_____ . . . gives a time line of measurement.

_____ . . . indicates who will carry out the evaluations(s) and how/why they were chosen.

_____ . . . states the criteria for success.

_____ . . . describes how the data will be collected.

_____ . . . explains the tests and instruments chosen to be utilized.

_____ . . . explains how the evaluation will be reported.

### The Budget . . .

_____ . . . breaks down the costs to be provided by the funding agency and those provided by other parties (PTA, school board, business, etc.).

_____ . . . matches the program objectives and activities.

_____ . . . can be detailed as to how a figure was arrived at.

_____ . . . includes all items asked for by the funding agency.

_____ . . . includes all items paid for by other sources (PTA, school board, business, etc.)

_____ . . . details fringe benefits, separate from salaries.

_____ . . . is sufficient to perform the tasks described in the activities and objectives.

# Grants for Schools—Part Three

## Table of Contents

# Analyzing Real Grant Proposal Forms

## The Intimidation Factor

### Afraid to Start?

The intimidation factor becomes an issue when you open your first RFP (Request For Proposal) and start to read. Although some of the newer, smaller ones are user-friendly and written in clear, easy-to-understand language, many are still reminiscent of the fine print on an insurance policy or a conditional sales contract for an automobile.

Since it is possible, in many cases, to download RFPs and print them from the World Wide Web, you may have also had to deal with problems caused by insufficient memory, inadequate software, and malfunctioning printers. Although it is fun to fool around with the *Web*, there is a lot to be said for the nice clear copy the funding agency will be glad to send to you through the mail. But, clear copy or not, afraid or not, if you are going to write a grant proposal, you have to start.

### You Will Never Be Afraid Again!

After you finish this part of the book, you will never be afraid again! (At least you will not be afraid of reading grant proposal instructions.) Four real grants are introduced in this section. They are presented here for analysis purposes only and are included to familiarize you with a variety of grant forms and proposal requirements. Starting with a small user-friendly grant and working your way up to more complicated grants, you are going to analyze forms, apply what you have learned, and take control.

For each grant presented, there are forms, questions, and annotated answer keys. Follow the instructions (a grant writing skill in itself) and watch your self-confidence grow. Pretend you are actually considering applying for the grants which you are reading. Study the grants and glean as much information as possible. Each section is a self contained test project. You may check your answers at the end of Part Three. You can write the requested information and answers directly in the book or you may wish to make copies. It may be a worthwhile exercise to share a grant set or two with the other members of the committee.

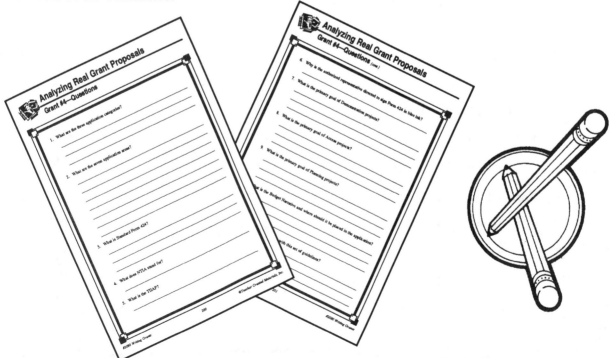

This grant is short and sweet!  Look over the materials on the next pages:

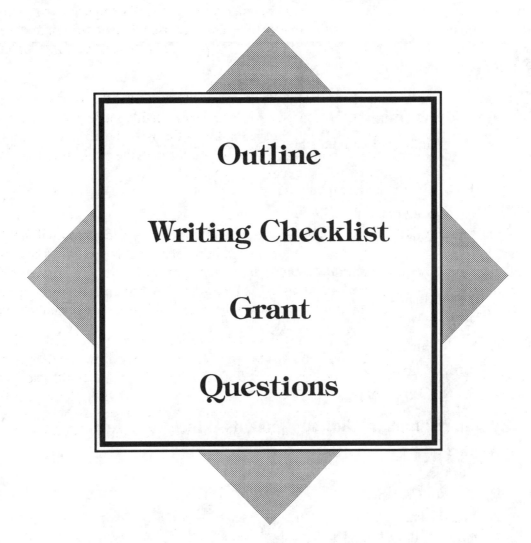

Outline

**Writing Checklist**

Grant

Questions

Write your answers on the pages or on copies of the pages.

(You could reproduce enough sets for everyone on the grant committee and compare answers.)

## When in Doubt, Call the Funder

If you need more information about anything, call the funder of the grant for clarification.  This suggestion will be repeated throughout the book.  When you come across the funder's information numbers, write them here.  Also, note the mailing address.

**Telephone number:** _____

**Fax number:** _____

**Mailing address:** _____

# Analyzing Real Grant Proposals

## Grant #1—Outline

Use the outline below to complete your Writing Checklist (pages 113 and 114) for grant #1.

---

### Outline

**I. Formatting Issues**

   A.  Determine the exact number of pages you must have or are allowed to have. Check:

      1.  Minimum number required (if there is one)

      2.  Maximum number allowed

      3.  Whether or not attachments are allowed

   B.  Check the page layout requirements.

      1.  Width of margins

      2.  Size of font

      3.  Justification

      4.  Spacing of lines

      5.  Numbering of pages

**II. Required and/or Allowed Elements Which May Include:**

   A.  Title

   B.  Abstract

   C.  Table of Contents

   D.  Introduction

   E.  Goals (vision/mission statement)

   F.  Statement of Needs

   G.  Objectives (stated in measurable terms)

   H.  Activities (how objective will be met)

   I.  Management

   J.  Personnel

   K.  Time Lines

   L.  Resources as Solutions

   M. Evaluation

   N.  Dissemination

   O.  Budget

   P.  Attachments

---

# Analyzing Real Grant Proposals

## Grant #1—Writing Checklist

Make photocopies of pages 111–114, and give a set to everyone involved in studying this grant proposal. Ask all of the participants to search the grant for the information listed below. It is important to know the guidelines of a grant so that you can follow them exactly. If the readers (scorers, judges) see that you did not follow the formatting requirements, they may be bound by the rules to throw out your proposal without even reading it.

## Formatting Issues

### A. Number of Pages

1. Minimum number required _____

2. Maximum number allowed _____

3. Attachments allowed (check one)  ❏ Yes   ❏ No

### B. Layout of Pages

1. Width of margins _____

2. Size of font _____

3. Justification _____

4. Spacing of lines _____

5. Numbering of lines _____

# Analyzing Real Grant Proposals

## Grant #1—Writing Checklist *(cont.)*

If an element in this grant is called something else than what is listed, note the term under the column entitled AKA (Also Known As).  You may need to refer to the definitions section of this book to do this.

| Elements | Required | Allowed | AKA |
|---|---|---|---|
| **Title** | | | |
| **Abstract** | | | |
| **Table of Contents** | | | |
| **Introduction** | | | |
| **Goal/Vision/Mission** | | | |
| **Statement of Needs** | | | |
| **Objectives** | | | |
| **Activities** | | | |
| **Management** | | | |
| **Personnel** | | | |
| **Time Lines** | | | |
| **Resources** | | | |
| **Evaluation** | | | |
| **Dissemination** | | | |
| **Budget** | | | |
| **Attachments** | | | |

(If attachments are allowed, what will they consist of?  Is there anything that you *cannot* attach?) _____

# INNOVATION GRANTS
# 1995-96 APPLICATION

## APPLICATION DEADLINE: THURSDAY, APRIL 25, 1996

## INNOVATION GRANTS PROFILE

The Innovation Grants program is sponsored by the Los Angeles Educational Partnership (LAEP), a nonprofit local education fund committed to improving student achievement in the Los Angeles community. The purpose of the Innovation Grants program is to support teachers to develop innovative instructional projects which will add vitality to student learning.

## GRANT ELIGIBILITY

Teams of teachers may apply for grants of up to $500 to support innovative classroom projects.
• Any Los Angeles Unified School District, Long Beach Unified School District, or Torrance Unified School District Pre-K through 12th grade classroom teacher may apply.
• All teachers must apply as part of a team (2 or more teachers working together).
• A teacher may apply for only one 1995-96 Innovation Grant.

## THE EDUCATION REFORM AGENDA

The Innovation Grants program seeks to incorporate the boarder school reform agenda at the classroom level. Successful applications will incorporate elements of education reform which directly impact student achievement. Elements of reform are articulated in the California State Curriculum Frameworks and other sources. They include, but are not limited to:

• student-centered learning
• hands-on lessons
• cross-age tutoring
• interdisciplinary
• emphasis on critical thinking & problem solving
• cooperative learning
• alternative modes of assessment
• parent, community, and/or business involvement

## 1995-96 FUNDING PRIORITIES: MATH AND SCIENCE

Major funding is provided by the Toyota USA Foundation for Toyota Innovation Grants in Math and Science. Applications which emphasize innovative math and/or science content and instruction are strongly encouraged. Applications in other content areas are eligible, but funds are limited. Toyota Innovation Grants in Math and Science are a major component of the country wide SMART (Science And Math Advancement Resources for Teachers) Initiative. For information about SMART, call 1-800-83-SMART.

## IMPORTANT DATES

• Applications must be received by LAEP **no later than 5:00 P.M. Thursday, April 25, 1996**.
• Grant notification will be mailed by June 14, 1996 for projects to begin in the Fall term.

## APPLICATION REQUIREMENTS

- Applications must be typed or computer printed in black ink only.
- You may separate the pages and staple them before sending.
- You may substitute a computer generated re-creation in lieu of this form, making certain to answer all of the questions in a similar format.
- Submit only Pages A through D, not the cover pages.
- No more than 4 pages will be accepted.

## SELECTION CRITERIA

- Learning objectives are clearly defined and have merit.
- Student activities are clearly described and brief examples are provided.
- Project is innovative and worthwhile.
- Elements of education reform are incorporated.
- Teacher collaboration and responsibilities are described.
- A brief time line is included.
- Budget items clearly support the objectives and activities.
- Application is easily understood by non-educators and is free of jargon.

## ELECTRONIC GRANT INFORMATION AVAILABLE

Beginning in January, 1996, LAEP will provide on-line grant writing information and updates. You may visit our LALCNet site now on the Internet. Our World Wide Web address is: http://www.lalc.k12.ca.us/
You may obtain and/or submit this application via e-mail at: grants@lalc.k12.ca.us.

## ADDITIONAL PROGRAM BENEFITS

- Grant checks are written directly to teachers.
- Recipients are honored at an annual Recognition Reception.
- A catalog is published describing all of the innovative projects for local and national distribution.

## INNOVATION GRANTS CONTRIBUTORS

| | | |
|---|---|---|
| Avery Dennison | IBM | Roth Family Foundation |
| Bank America Foundation | Long Beach Industry Education Council | Sony Pictures |
| Janie Block Education Foundation | MCA/Universal | Sidney Stern Foundation |
| Farmers Insurance Group | McMaster—Carr Supply Company | Torrance Chamber of Commerce |
| Great Western Financial Corporation | Milken Family Foundation | TRW—ECHO |
| IBJ Foundation | Prudential Insurance Co. of America | UNOCAL |
| | | J.B. and Emily Van Nuys Charities |

### Major funding is provided by the:

Toyota USA Foundation for Toyota Innovation Grants in Math & Science

## IN-KIND CONTRIBUTORS

- Los Angeles Unified School District • United Teachers Los Angeles • Long Beach Unified School District
  - Torrance Unified School District

In addition, the Innovation Grants program receives funding from many generous individuals.

## FOR FURTHER INFORMATION, CALL LAEP AT (213) 622-5237

PLEASE REVIEW APPLICATION REQUIREMENTS. APPLICATIONS MUST BE TYPED OR COMPUTER PRINTED.

**Project Title:**

**Content Area(s):**

**Education Reform Area(s):**

**Estimated Number of Students:**          **Grade Level(s):**          **Please circle one:  Elementary  Middle  Senior  Special Education**

## I.  PROJECT SUMMARY & OBJECTIVES: Briefly summarize your innovative project and state specifically what you want students to <u>know and be able to do</u> as a result of this grant.

## II. PROJECT DESCRIPTION & STUDENT ACTIVITIES: Clearly elaborate on your innovative project, providing examples of what students will be doing and learning.  Explain how the teacher applicants will collaborate and how you will incorporate elements of education reform.  Provide a brief, estimated timeline.  Describe how the budget items will be incorporated into your project.

**II. PROJECT DESCRIPTION & STUDENT ACTIVITIES,** continued

**III. BUDGET:** List materials, equipment, and/or resources needed to carry out your project. If the project costs more than $500, please describe any additional sources of funds or resources which will be used for this project. Applicants may not pay themselves, but there are no other budget restrictions.

<u>**ITEM DESCRIPTIONS**</u>                              <u>**COSTS**</u>

**TOTAL REQUEST** (*No More Than $500*)        $ _____
**IF APPLICABLE, OTHER FUNDING SOURCE(S)**    $ _____
**TOTAL PROJECT COST**                         $ _____

**School District:**

---

## Teacher Applicant #1

Name:

School Name:                                              School Schedule/Track:

School Address, City, Zip:

Home Address, City, Zip:

Home Phone:                    School Phone:              E-Mail Address (if any):

---

## Teacher Applicant #2  (A minimum of two teachers must apply)

Name:

School Name:                                              School Schedule/Track:

School Address, City, Zip:

Home Address, City, Zip:

Home Phone:                    School Phone:              E-Mail Address (if any):

---

## Teacher Applicant #3

Name:

School Name:                                              School Schedule/Track:

School Address, City, Zip:

Home Address, City, Zip:

Home Phone:                    School Phone:              E-Mail Address (if any):

---

## Teacher Applicant #4

Name:

School Name:                                              School Schedule/Track:

School Address, City, Zip:

Home Address, City, Zip:

Home Phone:                    School Phone:              E-Mail Address (if any):

---

• You may submit an additional page if your application includes more than 4 teachers•

Project Title:_____

Content Area(s): _____

Education Reform Area(s): _____

Amount Requested:     $ _____

Grade Level(s) Served: _____

Number of Classes to Participate: _____

Estimated Number of Students to Participate: _____

Briefly summarize your project (to be included in Grant Catalog if project is selected):

**APPLICATIONS MUST BE RECEIVED AT LAEP BY <u>5:00 P.M. ON APRIL 25, 1996.</u>**

**MAIL APPLICATIONS TO:**
Dianne Glinos, Grants Manager
Los Angeles Educational Partnership
315 W. Ninth Street, Suite 1110
Los Angeles, CA 90015

**OR SEND ELECTRONIC MAIL SUBMISSIONS TO:**
Our World Wide Web address is ttp://www.lalc.k12.ca.us/
You may obtain and/or submit this application via e-mail at
grants@lalc.k12.ca.us. Please read the directions on-line and e-mail
your application early to ensure receipt by the deadline.

**APPLICATIONS MAY <u>NOT</u> BE SUBMITTED BY FAX.**
**FOR FURTHER INFORMATION, CALL LAEP AT (213) 622-5237.**

•PLEASE MAKE AND RETAIN A COPY OF THIS APPLICATION FOR YOUR RECORDS•

# Analyzing Real Grant Proposals

## Grant #1—Questions

1. Can this grant application be submitted by FAX?  By e-mail?

   _____

2. What does LAEP stand for?

   _____

3. What is LAEP's World Wide Web address?

   _____

4. What is LAEP's e-mail Wide Web address?

   _____

5. When were applications for this grant to have been received?

   _____

6. How many teachers were required to apply for each grant?

   _____

7. How much money could be awarded for each proposal?

   _____

8. Who provided major funding for these grants?

   _____

9. What is SMART?

   _____

10. What was the limitation on the use of additional funds?

   _____

Still short but with a few surprises!  Look over the materials on the next pages:

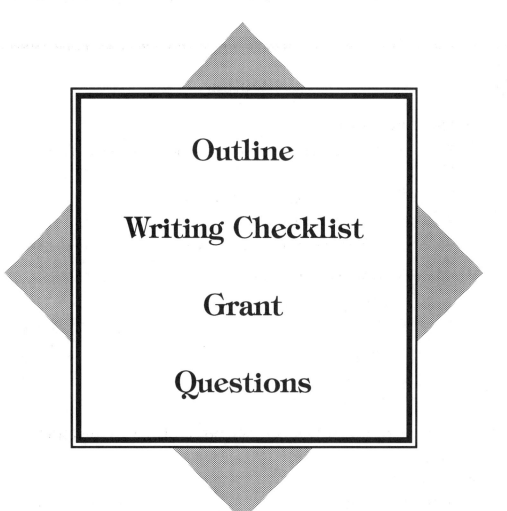

Outline

Writing Checklist

Grant

Questions

Write your answers on the pages or on copies of the pages.

(You could reproduce enough sets for everyone on the grant committee and compare answers.)

**When in Doubt, Call the Funder**

If you need more information about anything, call the funder of the grant for clarification.  This suggestion will be repeated throughout the book.  When you come across the funder's information numbers, write them here.  Also, note the mailing address.

**Telephone number:** _____

**Fax number:** _____

**Mailing address:** _____

# Analyzing Real Grant Proposals

## Grant #2—Outline

Use the outline below to complete your Writing Checklist (pages 124 and 125) for grant #2.

## Outline

### I. Formatting Issues

A. Determine the exact number of pages you must have or are allowed to have. Check:

   1. Minimum number required (if there is one)

   2. Maximum number allowed

   3. Whether or not attachments are allowed

B. Check the page layout requirements.

   1. Width of margins

   2. Size of font

   3. Justification

   4. Spacing of lines

   5. Numbering of pages

### II. Required and/or Allowed Elements Which May Include:

A. Title

B. Abstract

C. Table of Contents

D. Introduction

E. Goals (vision/mission statement)

F. Statement of Needs

G. Objectives (stated in measurable terms)

H. Activities (how objective will be met)

I. Management

J. Personnel

K. Time Lines

L. Resources as Solutions

M. Evaluation

N. Dissemination

O. Budget

P. Attachments

# Analyzing Real Grant Proposals

## Grant #2—Writing Checklist

Make photocopies of pages 122–125, and give a set to everyone involved in studying this grant proposal. Ask all of the participants to search the grant for the information listed below. It is important to know the guidelines of a grant so that you can follow them exactly. If the readers (scorers, judges) see that you did not follow the formatting requirements, they may be bound by the rules to throw out your proposal without even reading it.

## Formatting Issues

### A. Number of Pages

   1. Minimum number required _____

   2. Maximum number allowed _____

   3. Attachments allowed (check one)   ❑ Yes   ❑ No

### B. Layout of Pages

   1. Width of margins _____

   2. Size of font _____

   3. Justification _____

   4. Spacing of lines _____

   5. Numbering of lines _____

# Analyzing Real Grant Proposals

## Grant #2—Writing Checklist *(cont.)*

If an element in this grant is called something else than what is listed, note the term under the column entitled AKA (Also Known As).  You may need to refer to the definitions section of this book to do this.

| Elements | Required | Allowed | AKA |
|---|---|---|---|
| **Title** | | | |
| **Abstract** | | | |
| **Table of Contents** | | | |
| **Introduction** | | | |
| **Goal/Vision/Mission** | | | |
| **Statement of Needs** | | | |
| **Objectives** | | | |
| **Activities** | | | |
| **Management** | | | |
| **Personnel** | | | |
| **Time Lines** | | | |
| **Resources** | | | |
| **Evaluation** | | | |
| **Dissemination** | | | |
| **Budget** | | | |
| **Attachments** | | | |

(If attachments are allowed, what will they consist of?  Is there anything that you *cannot* attach?) _____

# The
# Hitachi
# Foundation

## Partnerships for Education and Economic Opportunity

### Request for Proposals (RFP) – Issued August 1, 1995

**Deadline for submitting proposals:** Friday, November 10, 1995

**Background**

In many communities, the current educational system faces great challenges in meeting youth's educational and work force preparation needs. Young people need both a strong academic background and work-related skills to perform the responsibilities of citizens and workers in a rapidly changing global society. Economic changes have essentially eliminated "lifelong" career paths and have vastly reduced employment opportunities for individuals with a high school diploma or less. The educational and economic challenges are particularly serious for youth from traditionally underserved populations, who are disproportionately placed on vocational tracks that lack academic breadth and rigor and often provide training for work in declining industries. The longterm goal must be to make our educational institutions and systems more effective in serving all youth. In the meantime, however, we cannot neglect those segments of the population that are presently not served effectively.

Many small programs are effectively preparing individuals for the workforce, and many communities have developed innovative collaborations between schools and businesses to strengthen students' education. Projects that stress "authentic" learning —learning that more readily permits students to relate their academic experience with the applied skills and information they need to pursue daily life and work— and that help prepare individuals for the work force, without focusing narrowly on one specific type of job, have proven to be successful. Employers, large and small, repeatedly focus on job skills such as literacy, communication, quantitative skills, problem solving, higher order thinking, independent learning, ability to work in teams, and "soft skills" such as appropriate dress and time management.

Along with schools, community organizations play key roles in work force development, serving as bridges for youth and filling critical training and educational gaps. While they have become critical in addressing the needs of underserved youth, these organizations frequently offer programs that are either too industry specific or too general, in that the learning does not easily translate into specific job skills. These programs also frequently serve only small numbers of youth.

**1509 22nd Street, NW • Washington, DC 20037-1037 • 202.457.0588 • Fax: 202.296.1098**

Significant issues of scale, impact, and comprehensiveness of educational and work force preparation cannot be resolved without further integration and collaborative effort between communities, agencies, formal education, and businesses. How can a program that serves 15 youth effectively serve a larger number without compromising program quality or outcomes? How can a program focusing on a given set of job skills be broadened through collaboration to offer a wider range of academic and work-related skills and information? How can community partners, such as businesses, community organizations and schools, be involved in more significant and longterm exchange of experience, knowledge, strategic thinking, and resources to enhance program scope and effectiveness?

**Programs to be funded**

This initiative seeks to stimulate the establishment, strengthening and/or expansion of collaborative efforts—involving community members and organizations, educational institutions, and businesses or other work places—to enhance the academic achievement and economic opportunities of youth underserved by formal academic and vocational programs.

For example, an agency (or a collaboration of two or more agencies) with a track record in work or career-related programs for youth might join with the high school and local employers to determine the employment trends and community issues, identify community resources available to strengthen students' preparation for future education and employment opportunities, and prepare a coordinated plan of services and curricula within which students can choose various paths and receive strong academic and work force preparation.

Proposed projects should:
- Involve formal, longterm, and substantive involvement and commitment from all partner institutions, as well as youth, parents, and community members. The particular elements funded by this grant should be part of a larger, longer-term plan that includes resource commitments from other partners for at least the term of that plan. (The proposal may include the development of such a plan.)
- Define education and work force development goals collaboratively and design a coordinated plan to achieve them.
- Integrate academic and job-training elements (defined above) in a manner that allows participants to choose among options and prepare them for an evolving employment market.
- Identify barriers to these types of collaborations and effective strategies for overcoming these barriers.
- Document and articulate the models and lessons learned in ways that encourage and enable other organizations and institutions to adopt and adapt such programs and strategies (through manuals, articles, workshops, etc.).

**Eligibility**

The Hitachi Foundation invites proposals from nonprofit, community organizations working on education and work force development issues with youth—middle school through the age of 25—from underserved populations—communities of color and low-income communities. Organizations or projects are not required to work with this full age range. The Foundation will not accept proposals from individual schools, school districts, colleges or universities, or state departments or boards of education. Ideally, the Foundation seeks organizations with collaborative links with schools, higher education institutions, or local businesses; but will consider independent efforts which are effective yet limited in scope, if the organization commits and has the capacity to involve other institutions and generate support to enhance the program and make it more self-sustaining over the long term. The proposed project must represent a critical intervention that takes the program to a new level of effectiveness.

**Project Terms**

The Foundation will consider projects of 2–5 years in length. The Foundation expects to provide individual grants totalling $100,000–$300,000 for the full project term. Full project budgets are expected to be larger, with the inclusion of additional funds and in-kind resources from partners and other sources. The Foundation expects to make grants to 4–6 organizations, diverse in location, character of collaboration, person, stages of program development, and methods in achieving program goals. To increase the learning potential across the cluster of grants made, formal exchange will occur between grantees within the cluster through convenings and other Foundation activities in which grantees will be expected to participate. The Foundation envisions two or more convenings, and will cover all associated costs of participation. Based on the experience with this RFP, the Foundation will decide whether to issue a similar RFP in the future. Grantees selected will be responsible for preparing interim and final reports detailing the program and financial status and outcomes. Reporting and payment schedules will be negotiated after grant approval.

Proposals will be reviewed and evaluated on the basis of the following criteria:

**Selection criteria and process**

- Identification of target population and specific programming goals related to academic and economic opportunities of the population; innovation and comprehensiveness of proposed activities, and potential to advance current practice.
- Effective program experience, capacity to deliver the target outcomes, and potential for significant, longterm impact on individuals and collaborating organizations.
- Experience with successful implementation of community, school, or business programs on education and workforce issues with the target population; and depth and range of networks for recruiting participants.

- Experience with collaborative efforts; evidence of partnership in program design, implementation, and evaluation; evidence of resources and interest (community, school, and corporate) leveraged in support of project goals and activities.
- Long-term commitment of significant support and active involvement from other partner(s) and evidence of sustainability of support.
- Feasibility and cost-effectiveness of project budget and activities.
- Quality of plans to evaluate the project's collaboration and impact.
- Evidence of diversity of perspective, person, network, and experience.

Foundation staff will review all proposals, and may enlist outside readers for additional comment. Top candidates will be asked to provide clarification or additional information approximately six weeks after the proposal deadline, and site visits by Foundation staff may also be conducted. Final approval of grants will be made by The Hitachi Foundation Board of Directors.

**How to apply**          Proposals should include the following materials:

- Completed cover sheet (form attached).

- A 4-6 page description (single or double-spaced) of the project including:

  - Brief description of the organization's philosophy of, knowledge of, and experience with education and work force development issues.
  - Evidence of impact from these past or current programs and the criteria for measuring that impact. If longitudinal impact data exist, please attach (not a requirement for funding).
  - For proposed activities, a description of target population, project goals and objectives, specific activities, specific educational and job-related content, and rationale. If related to existing programs and collaborations, describe the relationship of existing and proposed activities and how the proposed project will move current efforts forward.
  - Description of the target population and its size, and the specific challenges and issues it faces.
  - Plans to address issues of scale (expanding program impact and scope) and the obstacles, implications, and opportunities involved with these plans.
  - Description of past collaborations with education and/or corporate partners, if any, and commitments from such partners for the current proposal.
  - Details of existing or planned means of financial and programmatic sustainability beyond the funding provided by this grant.
  - Proposed evaluation criteria for the project.
  - Statement of organizational mission and capacity, including current programs, organization's operating budget, and staff.

■ Attachments:

- Timeline for the proposed activities.
- Overall project budget, with expenses itemized according to the proposed activities and personnel. Differentiate proposed funding from The Hitachi Foundation and include cash, in-kind, and other support (requested/committed) from other sources.
- Primary project personnel and brief qualifications.
- Letters of commitments from education, business, and community collaborators.
- Copy of 501(c)(3) tax exempt notification letter.

**Send proposals to:** **Partnerships for Education and Economic Opportunity**
**The Hitachi Foundation**
**1509 22nd Street N.W.**
**Washington, DC 20037-1073**
**No proposals will be accepted by fax.**

**Timetable**

| | |
|---|---|
| Friday, November 10, 1995 | Deadline for receipt of proposals. |
| Late December, 1995 | Notification of proposal status, full proposals solicited from top candidates; possible site visits. |
| Late January, 1996 | Deadline for submitting full proposals. |
| Mid-April, 1996 | Notification of grant decisions. |

**For more information**

Contact: Jeannette Rogers, Program Assistant, The Hitachi Foundation
202/457-0588, ext. 509

**The Hitachi Foundation**

In November of 1985, Hitachi, Ltd. of Tokyo established The Hitachi Foundation in Washington, DC, as a nonprofit, philanthropic organization with a mission to promote social responsibility through effective participation in a global society.

The Foundation seeks to build the capacity of all Americans, particularly those underserved by traditional institutions, to address the multicultural, community, and global issues facing them. The Foundation also seeks to engage Hitachi companies with critical social issues. The Foundation program emphasizes issues of diversity, multiculturalism, youth service, collaboration, corporate responsibility, and effective participation in a global society.

The Foundation does not accept unsolicited proposals. To identify projects to support, the Foundation issues requests for proposals (RFPs), develops collaborative projects, convenes grantees, undertakes program related investments, and disseminates program results. Information on current Foundation RFPs, funding guidelines and restrictions, and other initiatives is available through our "Fax on Demand System" accessible by telephone through (202) 457-0588 ext. 551.

## Partnerships for Education and Economic Opportunity Proposal Cover Sheet
Please attach the completed sheet to your proposal.  Copies are acceptable.

Organization Name _____

Address _____

City _____ State _____ Zip Code _____

Telephone _____ Fax _____

Contact Person _____ Title _____

Estimated Project Dates, Beginning: _____ Ending: _____

Total Project Budget: _____

     Amount Requested from The Hitachi Foundation: _____

     Amount Committed from Other Sources: _____

     Amount Pending from Other Sources: _____

Names of Collaborating Organizations: _____

_____

Geographic Area(s) Served by Project: _____

_____

Primary Target Population(s): _____

_____

Please identify from what source you first learned of this RFP. _____

Please state how you received the RFP document itself. _____

Please comment on the format and clarity of this RFP. _____

_____

Please comment on any other aspect of the RFP and its application procedures. _____

_____

Proposals must be received at the Foundation by November 10, 1995.

Please send completed cover sheets and proposals to:
Partnerships for Education and Economic Opportunity
The Hitachi Foundation
1509 22nd Street NW
Washington, DC 20037-1073

<u>Check contents enclosed:</u>

_____ Cover sheet
_____ 4-6 page proposal
_____ Attachments

# Analyzing Real Grant Proposals

## Grant #2—Questions

1. What is the dollar amount of the grants The Hitachi Foundation expects to fund?

   _____

2. How many grants does The Foundation expect to make?

   _____

3. What qualities will the organizations receiving funding have?

   _____

4. Does the Hitachi foundation fund individual schools?

   _____

5. What is the mission statement of The Hitachi Foundation?

   _____

6. Why are there two deadline dates for submitting proposals?

   _____

7. Who is the contact person for grant information?

   _____

# Analyzing Real Grant Proposal Forms

## Grant #3

This grant is very long; very federal. Look over the materials on the next pages:

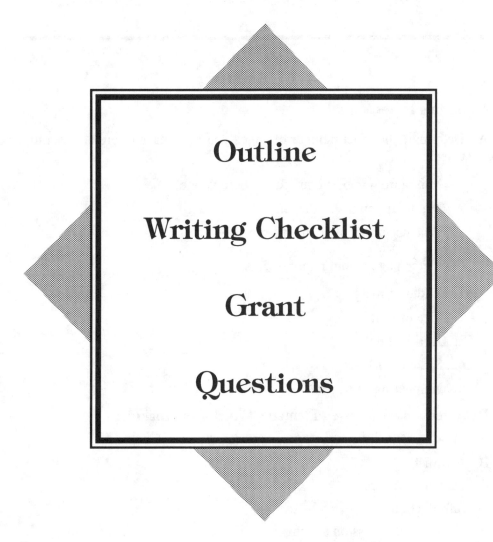

Outline

Writing Checklist

Grant

Questions

Write your answers on the pages or on copies of the pages.

(You could reproduce enough sets for everyone on the grant committee and compare answers.)

### When in Doubt, Call the Funder

If you need more information about anything, call the funder of the grant for clarification. This suggestion will be repeated throughout the book. When you come across the funder's information numbers, write them here. Also, note the mailing address.

Telephone number: _____

Fax number: _____

Mailing address: _____

# Analyzing Real Grant Proposals

## Grant #3—Outline

Use the outline below to complete your Writing Checklist (pages 135 and 136) for grant #3.

**Outline**

**I. Formatting Issues**

   A. Determine the exact number of pages you must have or are allowed to have. Check:

      1. Minimum number required (if there is one)

      2. Maximum number allowed

      3. Whether or not attachments are allowed

   B. Check the page layout requirements.

      1. Width of margins

      2. Size of font

      3. Justification

      4. Spacing of lines

      5. Numbering of pages

**II. Required and/or Allowed Elements Which May Include:**

   A. Title

   B. Abstract

   C. Table of Contents

   D. Introduction

   E. Goals (vision/mission statement)

   F. Statement of Needs

   G. Objectives (stated in measurable terms)

   H. Activities (how objective will be met)

   I. Management

   J. Personnel

   K. Time Lines

   L. Resources as Solutions

   M. Evaluation

   N. Dissemination

   O. Budget

   P. Attachments

# Analyzing Real Grant Proposals

## Grant #3—Writing Checklist

Make photocopies of pages 133–136, and give a set to everyone involved in studying this grant proposal. Ask all of the participants to search the grant for the information listed below. It is important to know the guidelines of a grant so that you can follow them exactly. If the readers (scorers, judges) see that you did not follow the formatting requirements, they may be bound by the rules to throw out your proposal without even reading it.

## Formatting Issues

### A. Number of Pages

1. Minimum number required _____

2. Maximum number allowed _____

3. Attachments allowed (check one)  ❏ Yes     ❏ No

### B. Layout of Pages

1. Width of margins_____

2. Size of font _____

3. Justification _____

4. Spacing of lines_____

5. Numbering of lines _____

# Analyzing Real Grant Proposals

## Grant #3—Writing Checklist *(cont.)*

If an element in this grant is called something else than what is listed, note the term under the column entitled AKA (Also Known As).  You may need to refer to the definitions section of this book to do this.

| Elements | Required | Allowed | AKA |
|---|---|---|---|
| Title | | | |
| Abstract | | | |
| Table of Contents | | | |
| Introduction | | | |
| Goal/Vision/Mission | | | |
| Statement of Needs | | | |
| Objectives | | | |
| Activities | | | |
| Management | | | |
| Personnel | | | |
| Time Lines | | | |
| Resources | | | |
| Evaluation | | | |
| Dissemination | | | |
| Budget | | | |
| Attachments | | | |
| (If attachments are allowed, what will they consist of?  Is there anything that you *cannot* attach?) _____ | | | |

# Teaching with Technology

**A National Endowment for the Humanities Special Opportunity**
**Initial Deadline: April 5, 1996**

Following the initial deadline, applications for Teaching with Technology may be submitted against the following regular program deadlines:

| | |
|---|---|
| Humanities Focus Grants | September 16, 1996; January 15, 1997 |
| Other Education Development & Demonstration Projects | October 1, 1996; October 1, 1997 |
| National Summer Institutes & Seminars | March 1, 1997;March 1, 1998 |

**Mailing Address for Applications**

Division of Research and Education, Room 302
National Endowment for the Humanities
1100 Pennsylvania Avenue, N.W.
Washington, DC 20506

To receive a hard copy of these guidelines and forms write to:
National Endowment for the Humanities
Public Information Office, room 402
1100 Pennsylvania Avenue, NW
Washington, DC 20506
or e-mail your request to: info@neh.fed.us

NEH will not accept applications sent via FAX machine or electronic mail.

## In this file:

- Teaching with Technology
- Becoming a Grantee
- The Application
- Budget Instructions
- Checklist

# Teaching with Technology

The National Endowment for the Humanities announces a special, three-year opportunity to support Teaching with Technology projects to strengthen education in the humanities by developing and using information technologies. Electronic technologies—including digital audio, video and imaging, hypertext and hypermedia, video-conferencing, speech processing, the Internet, and World Wide Web sites—can enable teachers to draw on newly accessible resources and to engage their students in active learning and higher-level thinking.

This Special Opportunity seeks projects of national significance that will extend these benefits to a broad range of those studying the humanities disciplines in schools, colleges, and universities.

Following the initial deadline, applications for Teaching with Technology will be accepted through several of the regular programs of the <u>Division of Research and Education.</u>

# GOALS

- o To increase the number and usefulness of technological resources with rich, high-quality humanities content, particularly for schools and colleges.

- o To improve the effectiveness of such resources by shaping them around sophisticated, creative, and engaging approaches to learning and by testing them in classrooms.

- o To increase significantly the number of teachers who can integrate such humanities materials into their daily teaching.

# WHAT ARE THE HUMANITIES?

The act that established the National Endowment for the Humanities says, "The term 'humanities' includes, but is not limited to, the study of the following: language, both modern and classical; linguistics; literature; history; jurisprudence; philosophy; archaeology; comparative religion; ethics; the history, criticism and theory of the arts; those aspects of social sciences which have humanistic content and employ humanistic methods; and the study and application of the humanities to the human environment with particular attention to reflecting our diverse heritage, traditions, and history and to the relevance of the humanities to the current conditions of national life."

# TYPES OF PROJECTS

Projects should address specific humanities topics and generate nationally significant resources, materials, and opportunities for enhanced humanities teaching and learning that can serve a wide and varied audience.

The Endowment seeks proposals (1) to develop new educational materials, (2) to field test and prepare classroom applications of new and existing materials, and (3) to enable school and college teachers to integrate new materials and approaches into their teaching. Proposals may focus on a single one of these categories or on combinations of them. Proposals involving school teachers and those aiming to enhance K-12 education are especially encouraged.

## 1) Materials Development

Projects to plan and design interactive educational software with excellent humanities content.

*Examples:*

*Seeking to apply new understandings of second language acquisition to intermediate and advanced level Spanish students, an association of high school Spanish teachers collaborates with a software developer to create a CD-ROM that simulates a visit to a Latin American city where students investigate the theft of an early colonial manuscript from a local museum. The program involves maps and views of the city, images of the museum and its galleries, and a series of Spanish speakers with whom the students interact. Using interviews with museum guards, curators, and local police, as well as literary and historical evidence, students travel through the city collecting information that helps them track down the thieves. During the investigation, students submit oral and written reports, which can be accessed by fellow students and the teacher. In addition to texts, videos, and illustrative materials, the CD-ROM includes a Spanish language dictionary, as well as other tools such as a note pad and indices.*

*A group of college teachers of the history of science creates a World Wide Web site for teaching resources. The site provides texts and translations, reference materials, simulations of historic observations and experiments, model course syllabi, a series of curricular modules, links to other Web resources, and information about activities that enhance student exploration of specific topics within this field. Among the resources available on the Web site are newly digitized records including writings of nineteenth century evolutionary biologists and early astronomical treatises going back to classical times. The site also will be called to the attention of high school teachers of physics, chemistry, and biology who seek to provide greater context for the science they teach.*

## 2) Field Testing and Classroom Applications

Projects that design and field-test innovative classroom uses of existing materials or those being developed.

*Examples:*

*A group of high school and college teachers of U.S. History field-test possible uses of an on-line data base including such records as United States Census Reports. In addition to testing in small-group projects and individual students research in their own U.S. history classes, the group assembles a network of teachers from across the country to develop and use the applications. The teachers arrange to share what they learn with the designers of the data base.*

*Faculty members from a regional consortium of higher education institutions, all of which require undergraduates to read selected texts from classical Greece, conduct two-week summer workshops and follow-up sessions during two successive academic years. During the summer workshops, they design course exercises and assignments using the computer program Perseus, a database that includes the texts of classical works, archaeological and historical images, and related information. During the academic years following the workshops, they will pilot the new course materials and evaluate and refine them while maintaining contact through an Internet bulletin board.*

## 3) Teacher Preparation

Projects that enable school and college teachers to integrate specific technologically innovative humanities materials and approaches into their teaching, and that promote collaboration among teachers working in these areas. These projects may involve collaborative projects among teachers in the same or neighboring institutions or national summer institutes.

*Examples: An archaeologist who is conducting a comprehensive research project in a district that contains the remains of prehistoric Native American villages, a seventeenth-century Spanish settlement, and an antebellum plantation conducts a year-long electronic workshop for school teachers in the metropolitan area around her university. The teachers participate in a series of excavations via the Internet and the World Wide Web. Through observations and descriptions delivered over the Internet as they occur, the teachers follow the progress of the excavations and also have access to records and archives of the archaeological digs; The World Wide Web site provides illustrative materials from the project, as well as links to related archaeological, historical, and curricular resources. On a series of moderated bulletin boards and monthly face-to-face meetings, the participating teachers, divided into grade level clusters, develop course materials derived from the project, which are then posted on the Web site to serve as a national resource.*

*A professor of English literature directs an NEH national summer institute on Shakespeare in performance for twenty-five college teachers. The residential five-week institute is held at a West Coast university that has previously established a comprehensive humanities computing center. Institute participants investigate the relationship between performance and interpretation, using a series of CD-ROMs containing the texts of Shakespearean plays and recordings of multiple performances of each play drawn from digitized versions of existing videos. As an adjunct to the institute, the group uses video- and tele- conferencing to link participants with a director and actors who are preparing a production of Hamlet for the annual Shakespeare festival in Stratford, Connecticut. During the academic year following the institute, the participants will collaborate through a continuing electronic discussion—accessible to others—of how the study of performance is illuminating their students' understanding of specific Elizabethan dramas.*

The examples above are based on several projects already funded by NEH. Applicants should be as creative as possible in proposing the use of newer technologies, and developing innovative strategies for using technology in humanities teaching.

## WHAT ARE THE CRITERIA FOR EVALUATING APPLICATIONS?

Teaching with Technology proposals are subject to three general criteria of evaluation: intellectual quality, potential for useful results, and feasibility.

- o Is the intellectual quality of the project excellent? Is its intellectual rationale clear and persuasive? Does the project engage an important humanities topic or text? Does it draw on sound humanities research? Is its approach thoughtful and stimulating? Does the project address effectively the pertinent issues of teaching and learning in this subject area?

- o Is the project worth doing? Is it likely to result in better humanities learning for students? Will it have lasting and far-reaching results? Will the project evaluation be thoughtful and informative? Will the results of the project be disseminated to those who will find them useful? Is the project budget reasonable in view of the likely results?

- o Is the project feasible? Are its activities well planned and described in adequate detail? Are the personnel well qualified to carry out their proposed responsibilities? Is it well suited to its institutional setting? Do letters from visiting scholars, technology consultants, or other experts demonstrate interest and commitment? Are the plans for administration sound? Is there evidence of a sufficient level of commitment and support by the participating institutions?

# BECOMING A GRANTEE

## SUBMITTING AN APPLICATION

After reading these guidelines, a potential applicant may wish to telephone a division program officer to discuss the proposed project. The program officer will determine the eligibility of a proposed project and assess its likely strengths and weaknesses. The potential applicant may also wish to submit a draft of the proposal for further review by a program officer before the formal application deadline. Although review of a written draft is not required, many applicants report that they have benefited from such consultations with division staff. Drafts should be submitted as early as possible. The staff cannot promise to review drafts received less than two weeks before the deadline.

The applicant should submit the completed proposal on the official application forms by the deadline. Once a proposal has been formally submitted, staff members are not permitted to discuss its status with the applicants until the conclusion of the review process.

Receipt of applications will be acknowledged by post card within three weeks. Applicants who have filed by the receipt deadline and who do not receive such an acknowledgment should call or write the Endowment as soon as possible. Applicants will receive formal notification once a final decision on the proposal has been reached.

Staff . . . . Telephone: 202/ 606-8373, Fax: 202/ 606-8394, E-Mail: education@neh.fed.us
Director: James Herbert
Deputies to the Director: Candace Katz, Kenneth Kolson

Education Development and Demonstrations, 202/ 606-8380
Program Officers: Ralph Canevali, Janet Edwards, Judith Jeffrey-Howard, Peter Losin, Frederick Winter

Seminars and Institutes, 202/ 606-8493
Program Officers: Thomas Adams, Barbara Ashbrook, David Coder Michael Hall

## REVIEW OF APPLICATIONS

Each Endowment application is assessed first by knowledgeable persons outside the agency who are asked for their judgements about the quality and significance of the proposed project. About 1,200 scholars, professionals in the humanities, and other experts serve on approximately 225 panels throughout the course of a year. Panelists represent a diversity of disciplinary, institutional, regional, and cultural backgrounds. In some programs the judgement of panelists is supplemented by individual reviews solicited from specialists who have extensive knowledge of the specific subject area of technical aspects of the applications under review.

The advise of evaluators is assembled by the staff of the Endowment, who comment on matters of fact or on significant issues that would otherwise be missing from the review. These materials are then forwarded to the National Council on the Humanities, a board of twenty-six citizens nominated by the President of the United States and confirmed by the Senate. The National Council meets three times each year to advise the Chairman of the Endowment. The Chairman, who is appointed for a four-year term by the President with the consent of the Senate, takes into account the advice provided by this review process and, by law, makes the final decision about funding. For the initial Teaching with

Reapplication is always possible, and failure to gain support in one competition does not prejudice an applicant's chances in future competitions. Applicants may, by submitting a written request, obtain detailed information about the evaluation of the proposal. The Endowment respects the confidentially of applicants and of the authors of specific reviews.

# TYPES OF GRANT SUPPORT

## Available Funding

The size of grants is consistent with such factors as the scope of the project and the number of participants. The Endowment anticipates that its contribution to grants for Teaching with Technology will range from $25,000 to $250,000. Applicants are encouraged to supplement this support with third party participation and with institutional cost sharing. Applicants should consult the sample budget as well as the budget instructions for additional information about the kinds of support available.

The Endowment supports projects with outright funds, matching funds, and a combination of the two.

Outright Funds

> Outright funds are awarded by the Endowment to support approved projects and are not contingent on additional fund raising by the grantees.

Matching Funds

> Matching funds, by contrast, require a grantee to secure gift funds from third parties before federal funds are awarded. Matching grants are made by the Endowment on a one-to-one basis and are intended to stimulate private support for projects in the humanities.

Because matching awards enable the Endowment to provide support to a greater number of significant but often costly projects, applicants are encouraged to request complete or partial support in the form of matching grants. Whenever possible, applicants requesting matching funds should identify potential sources of gift funds at the time they submit an application to the Endowment. (Please see note on eligible gifts and donors.)

## Cost Sharing

Applicants institutions are encouraged to share project expenses. Cost sharing consists of the cash contributions made to the project by the applicant institution and third parties, as well as third party in-kind contributions, such as donated services and goods. Applicants are especially encouraged to find sources of in-kind donations of hard and softwares that might serve the requirements of their projects. Cost sharing includes gift money that may be raised to release federal matching funds. Normally, the Endowment's contribution to Teaching with Technology projects will not exceed eighty-five percent of total project costs.

## Combined Funds

Applicants may request a combination of outright and matching funds from the Endowment. For example, if a project will cost $100,000 and the applicant will contribute $20,000 directly to the project's cost and expects to receive an additional $10,000 from an eligible third-party donor, the applicant should request $10,000 in matching funds. The balance of the project's cost ($60,000) may be requested in outright funds. The gifts raised in order to obtain the match should be included in the proposed budget as a component of the institution's cost-share. The total cost-share shown would then be $30,000.

The Endowment may offer funding at a different level from that requested. In some instances, the Endowment may offer matching funds only, or it may offer a combination of matching and outright funds in response to a request for outright funds.

## GRANT PERIOD

The grant period encompasses the entire period for which Endowment funding is requested in the application. All project activities and the expenditure of project funds, that is grant funds and cost-sharing contributions, must occur during the grant period.

The maximum period for which funding may be requested in an application is three years.

## GRANTEE RESPONSIBILITIES

If funding is approved by the Endowment, the applicant organization will be responsible for ensuring that the grant is administered in accordance with the following provisions.

- Project activities are to be carried out in accordance with the schedule provided in the approved application.
- Changes in the scope and objectives of the project may not be made without prior Endowment approval.
- The replacement of the project director, the co-director, or other professional staff members who are specifically named in an award notice requires prior Endowment approval.
- The grantee must have a financial management system that records separately within its general accounting system the receipt and disbursement of grant funds and cost-sharing contributions and which monitors the expenditure of these funds against the approved budget.
- All commitments and obligations of grant funds and cost-sharing contributions are to occur during the grant period.
- Adequate documentation of the time spent by all project personnel on grant activities must be maintained by the grantee.
- All procurement transactions are to be conducted in a manner that provides, to the maximum extent practical, open and free competition; for purchases in excess of $100,000, any use of single source contracts must be fully justified and documented.
- Grantees receiving $25,000 or more in federal awards during their fiscal year are required to have an audit performed.
- Unless otherwise notified in writing, grantees must acknowledge Endowment support in all materials resulting from grant activities, and on all promotional materials related to the project and, in the case of materials development grants, its products.
- If a grantee earns income from grant activities or products that result from grant activities, the Endowment reserves the right to recover a portion of the program income.

# THE APPLICATION

A complete application consists of six parts: an NEH Application Cover Sheet, a table of contents, a one-page summary of the proposed project, a detailed narrative describing the proposed project, a project budget, and appendices.

In preparing an application, follow these general directions:
type (double-space) the application on white 8 ½" x 11" paper;

create margins and select a type face and size that allow reviewers to read the application easily;

label the appendices, refer to them clearly in the narrative, and number the pages of all appendices consecutively.

# OVERVIEW OF THE APPLICATION

**Application Cover Sheet**
See the <u>instructions</u> for completing the NEH Application Cover Sheet.

**Table of Contents**
List all sections, including appendices.

**One-Page Summary**
Briefly summarize the narrative (see below). This summary must be no more than one typed page in length, but may be single-spaced.

**Narrative Descriptive of the Project**
The narrative is an extended discussion of the project, its intellectual content, its activities, and its intended beneficiaries. It is the focal point at every stage of the review process. The narrative should not exceed twenty double-spaced pages. To be competitive, a proposal should address the six matters listed below:

1. Rationale

An intellectual rationale must be clearly articulated. Explain how accomplishing the project objectives will improve the quality of humanities education. Specifically, describe how the particular electronic resources and approaches to teaching and learning proposed in the project would improve education in the humanities subject matter under consideration.

Identify the intended beneficiaries of the project. If the immediate impact of a project will be confined to a single institution, or to several institutions that are clearly specified, explain how the project will serve as a development or demonstration project for other institutions and in other settings nationwide. In the context, discuss how the cost of adoption in terms of hardware requirements, training needs, or other considerations might affect widespread use of the proposed materials and approaches in the classroom.

2. Institutional Context

Where relevant, describe how the project relates to the institution where it will take place. Show how the resources of the applicant and other participating institutions support the project, and describe any previous efforts to address the issues and objectives of the proposed undertaking. Cite relevant electronic, computing, library, archival, and museum resources. Discuss resources— hardware, software, administrative support, user support, etc.—required to carry out the proposed project, as well as the resources that would help foster a sense of intellectual community. For residential institutes, living facilities should be described.

If the proposal is similar or related to a project previously funded by the Endowment, include a detailed evaluation of the initial project in an appendix. Explain how the second grant would augment the first. If more than a single institution is involved, describe any collaboration that has already taken place to achieve similar goals.

If the project involves more than one institution, the application should include in an appendix letters of commitment from each.

## 3. Content of the Project

Identify the central issue or guiding question of the project. Provide details about the topics, texts, other materials to be studied and/or developed, and the approaches to teaching and learning to be used, and explain the connections among them. A detailed list of resources should be included. If the project involves materials currently under copyright, the applicant should indicate what will be done to secure the necessary permission for use of the materials.

## 4. Project Staff and Participants

Identify those who will conduct and administer the project, define their roles, and state their qualifications for undertaking the specific responsibilities assigned to them. Applicants may also identify appropriately qualified consultants—including additional humanities scholars and technical specialists—and should describe their qualifications and their roles in the project. Applicants for materials development projects should assemble an advisory board, whose members should not all come from the same institution.

In an appendix include one-page resumes from the project director and all other scholars and other experts contributing to the project, along with letters of commitment from each. Where applicable, describe the nature of the commitment and duties of advisory board members.

For projects in which participants should be identified at the time of application, provide names and pertinent information in this section. Otherwise, describe the criteria and procedures by which they will be selected.

## 5. Evaluation

Include a specific evaluation plan that closely corresponds to the project's objectives. The plan should include formative and summative evaluation. Evaluation plans should describe the criteria by which the success of the project would be measured.

The evaluation of materials development projects should focus both on the software design and on its uses in the classroom. Describe the qualifications of external evaluators if they are to be used, and include in an appendix letters indicating their willingness to serve.

6. Follow-up and Dissemination

> Describe in detail how the benefits of the project would continue once project funding ends. Where pertinent, show how materials produced by a project or other results of broad significance would be made accessible nationwide and how the new materials or approaches to learning would serve as models for further development in teaching with technology. Discuss the resources — hardware, software, administrative support, user support, etc.,—required for any products or learning techniques to be used by a broad audience. Where appropriate, describe the potential for multi-platform compatibility (for example, between Mac and DOS systems) of the materials developed or field tested and any plans for accommodating rapid technological change (for example, migration of data from CD-ROM to a future medium).

## Project Budget
See the budget instructions.

## Appendices
Use appendices to provide supplementary but essential materials, such as work plans, lists of resources, permissions, technical specifications, syllabi, resumes, and letters of commitment. Appendices should include relevant and concisely presented information only. Each appendix should be identified clearly and listed in the Table of Contents. Pages of the appendices should be numbered consecutively. At appropriate places in the proposal narrative, references should be made to items included in the appendices.

## Certification Requirements
By signing and submitting a proposal the authorizing official of the applicant institution provides the applicable certifications. When a prospective applicant is unable to certify regarding the nondiscrimination statutes and implementing regulations, a drug-free workplace, or lobbying, that institution is not eligible to apply for funding from NEH. When an applicant is unable to certify regarding of federal status or debarment and suspension, an explanation must be attached to the proposal. The explanation of why the certification cannot be submitted will be consideration in connection with the NEH's funding determination. Failure to furnish a certification or an explanation shall disqualify the applicant from receiving an award from NEH.

The certifications are material representations of fact upon which reliance will be placed when the NEH determines to fund the application. If it is later determined that the applicant knowingly provided an erroneous certification or did not comply with the requirements, in addition to other remedies available to the federal government, the NEH may seek judicial enforcement of the certification (nondiscrimination statues); may terminate the award for cause or default (federal debt status and debarment and suspension); and may suspend payment, suspend or terminate the grant, or suspend or debar the grantee (drug-free workplace). Any grantee who fails to file a required certification shall be subject to a civil penalty of not less than $10,000 and not more than $100,000 for each failure.

In addition to the certification that the institution sponsoring the seminar must send to NEH, participants receiving stipends from the grant must also certify compliance with the regulations involving debarment and suspension. The certification is included as part of the NEH Summer Seminars Participant Application Cover Sheet, which can be found in the Summer Seminars Participant Guidelines.

The sponsoring institution must ensure that the application cover sheets from all selected participants include the appropriate certification statement and signature. These certifications should be read before signing Block 12 of the application cover sheet. Additional information on these certifications is available from the NEH Grants Office, room 310, Washington, D.C. 20506, (202) 606-8494.

**Privacy Act**

This information is solicited under the authority of the National Foundation on the Art and Humanities Act of 1965, as amended, 20 U.S.C. 956. The principle purpose for which the information will be used is to process the grant application. The information may also be used for statistical research, analysis of trends, and Congressional oversight. Failure to provide the information may result in the delay or rejection of the application.

# INSTRUCTIONS FOR COMPLETING THE NEH APPLICATION COVER SHEET

A standard cover sheet (available here with Adobe Acrobat Reader software) is required for applications to NEH. The following instructions explain how applicants to the special opportunity in Teaching with Technology in the Division of Research and Education Programs should complete the cover sheet. The Office of Management and Budget requires federal agencies to supply information on the time needed to complete forms and also to invite comments on the paperwork burden. NEH estimates the average time to complete this form is ten hours per response. This estimate includes the time for reviewing instructions; researching, gathering, and maintaining the information needed; and completing and reviewing the application. Please send any comments regarding the estimated completion time or any other aspect of this application, including suggestions for reducing the time needed to complete it, to the Director of the Office of Publications and Public Affairs, National Endowment of the Humanities, Washington, D.C. 20506; and to the Office of Management and Budget, Paperwork Reduction Project (3136-0134), Washington, D.C. 20503.

**Block 1**—Individual applicant or project director

Item a. Enter the name and mailing address of the person who will carry out the project or be chiefly responsible for directing it. (Information about an institution also is requested in Blocks 2, 11, and 12.)

Item b. In the space provided, enter the number corresponding to the project director's preferred form of address:

| | | |
|---|---|---|
| 1-Mr. | 3-Miss | 5-Professor |
| 2-Mrs. | 4-Ms. | 6-Dr. |

Item c. Enter the project director's full telephone number with area code and extension.

Whenever possible, specify a telephone number at which a message can be left.

Item d.  If possible, indicate the code for the appropriate major field from the list of Field of Project Categories and Codes on the reverse side of the Application Cover Sheet.

**Block 2**—Type of applicant
Check (b)

Identify type of institution—for example, educational institution (elementary/secondary, school district, two year college, four year college, etc.), religious organization, museum, historical society, government (state, local, etc.), public media (TV, radio, newspaper, etc.), library (public, research, etc.), center (advanced study, research, etc.)

Identify status as either private nonprofit or unit of state or local government.
Example: Type: Historical Society.  Status: Private Nonprofit.

**Block 3**—Type of application
Check appropriate type:

Item a.  New—applicants requesting a new period of funding, whether for an entirely new project or for a project funded by NEH for a previous period, should check this box.

Item b.  Supplement—applicants requesting additional funding during a current NEH grant should check this box.

**Block 4**—Program to which application is being made
In the space provided, enter Educational Development and Demonstration.

Under "Endowment Initiative," enter 03T.

**Block 5**—Requested grant period
Grant periods begin on the first day of the month and end on the last day of the month.  Project activities need not begin on the first day, but all project activities must take place within the requested grant periods.

**Block 6**—Project funding
Enter here the appropriate figures from page 4 of the NEH Budget Form, "Project Funding for Entire Grant Period."  Fill in lines (a) through (e); enter "0" for blank lines.

**Block 7**—Field of project
See the listing on the reverse side of the cover sheet for the category and code of the specific humanities field that best describes the content of the project.

**Block 8**—Descriptive title of project
Enter a brief title that clearly identifies the project and its humanities content.  This title should be informative to a nonspecialist.  NEH is obliged to be as clear as possible to the public about awards that it makes.  The descriptive title will be used for this purpose whenever possible, but the Endowment staff may assign a different working title of the project.

**Block 9**—Description of project
Provide a brief description of the proposed project.  Do not exceed the space provided.

**Block 10**—Will this proposal be submitted to another government agency or private entity for funding? This information is sought without prejudice to the application. NEH frequently cosponsors projects with other funding sources. If not applicable, indicate "N/A."

**Block 11**—Institutional data

Item a. Indicate the name of the institution and the city and state of its official mailing address.

Item b. Enter the institution's employer identification number.

Item c. Indicate the name and title of the person who is authorized to submit the application on behalf of the institution or organization and to provide the certifications required in Block 12.

Item d. Indicate the name, mailing address, form of address (see instructions for Block 1, Item b), and the telephone number of the person who will be responsible for the financial administration of the grant if the award is made. For example, at many universities the provost, vice president, president, or chancellor is the person "authorized" to submit an application (see Item c), but the actual administration of the project—such as negotiating the project budget or ensuring compliance with the terms and conditions of the award—is the responsibility of a grants or research officer. It is the latter person who should be listed here.

**Block 12**—Certification

The Endowment is required to obtain from all applicants certifications regarding federal debt status, debarment and suspension, and a drug-free workplace. Applicants requesting more than $100,000 in grant funds also must certify regarding lobbying activities and may be required to submit a "Disclosure of Lobbying Activities" (Standard Form LLL). Institutional applicants are required to certify that they will comply with the nondiscrimination statutes and their implementing regulations. These certifications and the accompanying instructions should be read carefully before the application cover sheet is signed because most of these certifications impose new responsibilities on successful applicants.

# BUDGET INSTRUCTIONS

The project budget must appear on the NEH Budget Form and must be prepared in accordance with the budget instructions. Additional explanation may be appended in a budget narrative. Before completing the budget form, review the information that pertains to the types of funds available, cost-sharing expectations, grant period definition, and grantee responsibilities, as well as the note concerning eligible gifts and donors. If you have questions after reading these guidelines and budget instructions, please contact a division program officer for advice. The division staff will provide guidance on preliminary budgets submitted with draft proposals.

**Requested Grant Period**

Grant periods begin on the first day of the month and end on the last day of the month. All project activities must take place during the requested grant period. For grant periods of longer than eighteen months, separate budgets for each twelve-month period of the project must be submitted.

## Project Costs

The budget should contain all costs related to the project. Therefore, it should include costs that will be supported by applicant or third party cash and in-kind contributions as well as those that will be charged to grant funds. All of the items listed, whether supported by grant funds or cost-sharing contributions, must be reasonable, necessary to accomplish project objectives, allowable in terms of the applicable federal cost principles, auditable, and incurred during the grant period. Charges to the project for items such as salaries, fringe benefits, travel, and contractual services must conform to the written policies and established practices of the applicant organization. When indirect costs are charged to the project, care should be taken that expenses included in the organization's indirect cost pool are not charged to the project as direct costs.

## 1. Salaries and Wages

This section should include all project personnel except participants and consultants who are not employees of the applicant institution. Calculations for faculty compensation should be based on a percentage of academic year or annual salary. The division does not support replacement teachers or compensate faculty members for performing their regular duties. Compensation for support staff may be calculated as a percentage of salary or based on an hourly rate.

For Materials Development and Field Testing and Classroom Applications Grants salary compensation should be shown in the project budget as follows:

- For Project Directors during the academic year: released time normally should not exceed one course (or 40% of course load, whichever is greater) per quarter or semester.

- For Project Directors during the summer: compensation is based on a percentage of their base academic year salary. For example, one month would equal one-ninth or 11.1% of a nine month academic year salary. Two co-directors would each receive 70% of this amount, based on their individual academic year salaries.

- For Higher Education faculty participants during the academic year: released time should normally not exceed one course per academic year.
- For school teacher and faculty participants during the summer: uniform stipends of no more than $500 per week may be charged.

- For Institutes: Directors of institutes receive compensation for the time they spend on planning, directing the institute during the summer, and conducting follow-up activities.

    For a five week institute: total compensation would normally be 25% of a base academic year salary.

    For a six week institute: total compensation would normally be 27.8% of a base academic year salary.
    For two co-directors: each would be compensated at 70% of the rates described above, based on their individual base academic year salaries.

Compensation may be greater if institutes require extensive follow-up activities or smaller if portions of the work will be carried out by an administrative assistant or project coordinator or by the other co-director. Justification for requests for additional compensation or for an unusually long or complex project must be provided in the budget narrative.

## 2. Fringe Benefits

Fringe benefits should be calculated only for those individuals listed under Salaries and Wages. Fringe benefits may include contributions for social security, employee insurance, pension plans, etc. Only those benefits that are not included in an organization's indirect cost pool may be shown as direct costs.

Depending on institutional practice, fringe benefits may or may not be calculated for summer stipends. Also, fringe benefits for support, administrative, and part-time personnel may be calculated at different rates than academic year employees. This should be reflected in the breakdowns shown on the budget form.

## 3. Consultant Fees

List those individuals who would contribute to the project as visiting lecturers, leaders of faculty study sessions, technical consultants, and external evaluators. The honoraria for visiting faculty and other consultants range from $250 to $350 per person per day or $1,250 per person per week, not including travel and subsistence costs. Travel and subsistence costs should be entered in budget section 4.

## 4. Travel

Travel and subsistence costs, including participant travel that occurs as part of a summer institute or collaborative project, should be entered in this section. Costs should be calculated in conformity with institutional policy. (However, room and board for participants in residential projects should be entered in budget section 7.) Less-than-first-class accommodations must be used and foreign travel must be undertaken on U.S. flag carriers when such services are available. Project directors will attend planning meetings at the Endowment's offices in Washington, D.C. Directors should budget for a two-day meeting in the fall of 1996.

## 5. Supplies and Materials

Include such items as stationery supplies, computer diskettes, books and CDs for participants, films, videotapes, hardware costing less than $5,000, and educational software. All must be essential to the project. See the section for Inadmissible Budget Items.

## 6. Services

Include items such as costs of photocopying, postage, long distance telephone, and the printing of publicity materials. If rental of equipment is proposed, enter it in this section of the budget form. (Equipment may be purchased only if rental costs exceed purchase price.) Large or expensive equipment rentals and purchases must be justified in the budget narrative. (See section 8 for treatment of equipment purchases.)

## 7. Other Costs

Participant Stipends: Stipends for participants not employed by the applicant institution should be listed here. Institutes provide participants with an allowance to defray the costs of room and board and a stipend of $250 per week. The host institution should provide project participants with arrangements and privileges appropriate to their status as visiting scholar/teachers. In the case of residential institutes, the host institution is required to allow participants to apply the room and board allowance to off-campus housing and meals. For projects in elementary and secondary education, applicants may charge the costs for support of school teachers participating in academic year follow-up activities.

Equipment: When an applicant proposes to charge the purchase of permanent equipment to a project, this expense should be included under "Other Costs." The applicant must demonstrate in the budget narrative that the purchase of permanent equipment is necessary to carry out the project and will be less expensive than rental. Permanent equipment is defined as an item costing more than $5,000 with an estimated useful life of more than one year. Equipment costing less than $5,000 may be purchased and itemized under Supplies and Materials.

## 8. Total Direct Costs

These are the costs of the project excluding indirect costs.

## 9. Indirect Costs (Overhead)

These are costs that are incurred for common or joint objectives and therefore cannot be readily identified with a specific project or activity of an organization. Examples of indirect cost items are the salaries of executive officers, the costs of operating and maintaining facilities including central computing facilities, local telephone service, office space and utilities, and accounting and legal services.

Indirect costs are computed by applying a federally negotiated indirect cost rate to a distribution base (usually the direct costs of the project, excluding institute participant stipends equipment, and subcontracts over $25,000). Organizations that wish to include overhead charges in the budget but do not have a current federally negotiated indirect cost rate or have not submitted a pending indirect cost proposal to a federal agency may choose one of the following options:

- a. The Endowment will not require the formal negotiation of an indirect cost rate, provided the charge for indirect costs does not exceed ten percent of direct costs, less distorting items (e.g., capital expenditures, participant stipends, major subcontracts), up to a maximum charge to the project, including cost-sharing, of $5,000 annually. (Applicants who choose this option should understand that they must maintain documentation to support overhead charges claimed as part of project costs.)

- b. If your organization wishes to use a rate higher than ten percent or claim more than $5,000 per year in indirect costs per year, an estimate of the indirect cost rate and the charges should be provided on the budget form. If your application is approved for funding, you will be instructed to contact the NEH Office of the Inspector General to negotiate an indirect cost rate.

### Budget Narrative

Include a brief budget narrative when costs are unusual or not easily related to the project narrative.

Clarification of salary items may be useful here. If released time from teaching duties is proposed, indicate clearly how it will be used. Justifications for large or expensive equipment rentals and purchases must be provided here.

## Inadmissible Budget Items

The following costs are not allowable and may not appear in project budgets:

The cost of replacement teachers or compensation for faculty members performing their regular duties.

The rental of recreational facilities and costs related to social events such as banquets, receptions, and entertainment.

Tuition fees for institute participants. Credit may be awarded to participants seeking it, however, at the discretion of the applicant institution. If any filing fee or tuition must be charged, it should be charged directly to those participants wishing to receive credit and should be fixed at the lowest possible rate. Such fees should not be deducted from the participants' stipends.

The division does not fund or accept as cost sharing the development of education technologies or materials that are solely pedagogical and do not concern specific academic content.

# Sample Budget Computations

Sample A: Materials Development Grant

| | | NEH Funds | Cost Sharing | |
|---|---|---|---|---|
| **1. Salaries and Wages** | | | | |
| Proj. Dir./Sr. Scholar | 33.3% @ $65,000 | $10,822 | $10,822 | $ |
| Sr. Tech. Producer | 33.3% @ $55,000 | $18,315 | | $ |
| Asst. Tech. Producer | 20% @ $27,000 | $ 5,400 | | $ |
| Programmer/Tech. Spec. | 40% @ $50,000 | $20,000 | | $ |
| Clerical | 10% @ $18,000 | $ 900 | $ 900 | $ |
| **2. Fringe Benefits** | 22% of $65,359 | $11,998 | $2,381 | $ |
| | 15% of $ 1,800 | $ 135 | $ 135 | $ |
| **3. Consultant Fees** | | | | |
| Advisory Bd. Scholars | 3% @ $300/9 days | $8,100 | | $ |
| Picture/Hist. Rshrs. | 2% @ $80/30 days | $4,800 | | $ |
| Graphics Designer | 30 hours/@ $150 | $4,500 | | $ |
| Legal Counsel | 20 hours/@ $200 | $4,000 | | $ |

**4. Travel**

| | no. of persons | total days | travel costs | + | subsistence costs | transport. = | | |
|---|---|---|---|---|---|---|---|---|
| City/City | (3) | (6) | $600 | | $1500 | $2,100 | | $ |
| City/ Wash., D.C. | (1) | (2) | $250 | | $450 | $700 | | $ |

| **5. Supplies and Materials** | | | |
|---|---|---|---|
| e.g. Optical Drive Cartridges/memory upgrades, etc. | $2,000 | | $ |
| Postage | $ 400 | | $ |
| Photocopying | $ 600 | | $ |

6. Services

| | | | |
|---|---|---|---|
| Permissions | $ 20,000 | | $ |
| Pressing CD-Roms | $ 800 | | $ |
| Phone | $ 350 | | $ |

7. Other Costs

| | | |
|---|---|---|
| New Equipment (In-kind Contribution) | $ 12,500 | $ |

8. Total Direct Costs — $115,920 — $26,738

9. Indirect Costs — 35.9% of $130,158 — $ 41,615 — $ 5,111 $

10. Total Project Costs (Direct and Indirect) — $157,535 — $31,849 $1

This sample budget shows all project personnel as employed by the grantee institution with remuneration listed under 1. Salaries and Wages. In the case of projects in which several institutions cooperate, compensation for those participants not employed by the grantee institution should be entered under 7. Other Costs.

### Sample B: Field Testing and Classroom Applications Grant

| | | NEH Funds | Cost Sharing |
|---|---|---|---|

1. Salaries and Wages

| | | NEH Funds | Cost Sharing | |
|---|---|---|---|---|
| Project Director | 25% (2-course release) | | | |
| | @ $45,000/academic yr. | $5,625 | $5,265 | $1 |
| | 1 summer mo. @ 11.1% | $2,498 | $2,497 | $ |
| Secretarial Support | 25% of $16,000/yr. | $4,000 | | $ |

2. Fringe Benefits

| | | NEH Funds | Cost Sharing | |
|---|---|---|---|---|
| | 11% of $16,245 | | $1,787 | $ |
| | 8% of $ 4,000 | $ 320 | | |

3. Consultant Fees

| | | NEH Funds | Cost Sharing |
|---|---|---|---|
| Humanities Scholars | 5% @ $ 350 | $1,750 | $ |
| Technical Consultant | 2% @ $ 350 | $ 700 | $ |
| Curriculum Consultant | 3% @ $ 350 | $1,050 | $ |
| Evaluator | 10% @ $ 250 | $2,500 | $ |

4. Travel

| | | | no. of<br>persons | total<br>days | travel<br>costs | + | subsistence<br>costs | = | transport. | | |
|---|---|---|---|---|---|---|---|---|---|---|---|
| City/City | (1) | (3) | $300 | $350 | | | | | $ 650 | | $ |
| City/City | (1) | (4) | $400 | $300 | | | | | $ 700 | | $ |
| City/City | (1) | (3) | $300 | $730 | | | | | $1,030 | | $ |
| City/City | (1) | (4) | $400 | $210 | | | | | $ 610 | | $ |
| City/<br>Wash., D.C. | (1) | (2) | $250 | $350 | | | | | $ 600 | | $ |

5. Supplies and Materials

| | NEH Funds | Cost Sharing | |
|---|---|---|---|
| Computer hardware/memory upgrades | $2,000 | $2,000 | $ |
| Site licenses for educational software | $1,500 | | $ |
| Computer disks 10 boxes @ $20 | $ 200 | | $ |
| Stationery | $ 100 | | $ |

| | | NEH Funds | Cost Sharing | |
|---|---|---|---|---|
| 6. Services | | | | |
| Printing | est. 5,000 copies @ $.40 | $2,000 | | $ |
| Photocopying | est. 2,500 copies @ $.10 | $250 | | $ |
| Videotaping | | $2,000 | | $ |
| 7. Other Costs | | | | |
| 8. Total Direct Costs | | $30,083 | $11,909 | $4 |
| 9. Indirect Costs | 30% of $41,992 | $9,025 | $3,573 | $1 |
| 10. Total Project Costs (Direct and Indirect) | | $39,108 | $15,482 | $5 |

| | | NEH Funds | Cost Sharing | |
|---|---|---|---|---|
| 1. Salaries and Wages | | | | |
| Project Director | 11.1% @ $38,000/academic yr. | $4,218 | | $ |
| Secretarial Support | 10% @ $14,000/yr. | | $1,400 | $ |
| 2. Fringe Benefits | | | | |
| | 11% of $4,218 | $ 464 | | $ |
| | 8% of $1,400 | | $ 112 | $ |
| 3. Consultant Fees | | | | |
| Consultant | 5 @ $250 per | $1,250 | | $ |
| Consultant | 3 @ $250 per | $ 750 | | $ |

4. Travel

|  | | | no. of total travel | subsistence | transport. | | | |
|---|---|---|---|---|---|---|---|---|
| | persons | days | costs | + | costs | = | | |
| Within City | (2) | (8) | $0* | $192 | | $432 | | $ |
| Wash., D.C. | (1) | (2) | $250 | $450 | | $700 | | $ |
| (Project Directors Meeting) | | | | | | | | |

| | | NEH Funds | Cost Sharing | |
|---|---|---|---|---|
| 5. Supplies and Materials | | | | |
| Books and Cds | 12 sets at $80 per | $ 480 | $480 | $ |
| Computer hardware/high speed modems | | $1,500 | $1,500 | $ |
| 6. Services | | | | |
| 7. Other Costs | | | | |
| Stipends to Participants | | | | |
| 12 x $50 x 15 half days | | $ 9,000 | | $ |
| 8. Total Direct Costs | | $18,794 | $3,492 | $1 |
| 9. Indirect Costs | 10% of $13,286 | $ 979 | $349 | $ |
| 10. Total Project Costs (Direct and Indirect) | | $19,773 | $3,841 | $2 |

*Subsistence not availble for in-city travel.

## Sample D: Institute

|  |  |  |  |  | NEH Funds | Cost Sharing |  |
|---|---|---|---|---|---|---|---|
| **1. Salaries and Wages** | | | | | | | |
| Project Director | | 22.2% @ $60,000/ academic yr. | | | $6,660 | $6,600 | $ |
| Assistant | | 20% @ $27,000/ academic yr. | | | $2,700 | $2,700 | $ |
| Secretarial Support | | 3 mo. x 100% @ $14,000/yr. | | | $1,750 | $1,750 | $ |
| **2. Fringe Benefits** | | | | | | | |
| | | 11% of $18,720 | | | $1,030 | $1,029 | $ |
| | | 8% of $3,500 | | | $ 140 | $ 140 | $ |
| **3. Consultant Fees** | | | | | | | |
| Professor | 3 | $250/da. | | | $ 750 | | $ |
| Professor | 5 | $250/da. | | | $1,250 | | $ |
| Professor | 3 | $250/da. | | | $ 750 | | $ |

### 4. Travel

| | no. of persons | total days | travel costs | + | subsistence costs | transport. = | | |
|---|---|---|---|---|---|---|---|---|
| City/City | (1) (3) | $300 | $730 | | $1,030 | | | $ |
| City/City | (1) (5) | $500 | $425 | | $ 925 | | | $ |
| City/City | (1) (3) | $300 | $300 | | $ 600 | | | $ |
| City/ Wash., D.C.* | (1) (2) | $ 250 | $ 500 | | $750 | $750 | | $ |
| Participants/City(25)** | (2) | $10,000 | | | $10,000 | | | $ |

| | | | NEH Funds | Cost Sharing | |
|---|---|---|---|---|---|
| **5. Supplies and Materials** | | | | | |
| Books and CDs | 25 sets of $90 per | | $2,250 | | $ |
| Films | 3 films of $75 ea rental | | $ 225 | | $ |
| **6. Services** | | | | | |
| Long Distance Telephone | est. 40 tolls @ $3 | | $ 120 | | $ |
| Photocopying | est. 2,500 copies @ $.10 | | $ 250 | | $ |
| Printing | 5,000 @ $.40 | | $1,000 | $1,000 | $ |
| Postage | 400 pieces @ $.25 | | $ 100 | | $ |
| Advertising | 3 journal notices @ $150 | | $ 450 | | $ |
| **7. Other Costs** | | | | | |
| Participant Stipends | 25 x $250 x 4 wks. | | $25,000 | | $ |
| Participants' Room & Board | 25 x $300 x 4 wks. | | $30,000 | | $ |
| **8. Total Direct Costs** | | | $87,730 | $13,279 | $1 |
| **9. Indirect Costs** | 48% of $46,009 | | $15,710 | $6,374 | $ |
| **10. Total Project Costs (Direct and Indirect)** | | | $103,440 | $19,653 | $1 |

* Project Directors Meeting

** Higher Education institutes only.  Elementary and Secondary Education
   institutes normally serve thirty-five participants.

# CHECKLIST FOR A COMPLETE APPLICATION PACKAGE

The application package sent to the division should contain twelve copies of the application itself, placed on top of these twelve copies should be the following separate documents.

- The completed NEH Application Cover Sheet with an original signature of the institution's authorizing official (Do not use black ink for signature)

- Three photocopies of the completed Application Cover Sheet

- Three photocopies of the one page summary of the project (may be single-spaced)

- The original completed NEH Budget Form

Each of the twelve copies of the application itself, placed underneath the separate documents in the application package, should be organized in the following way.

Twelve copies of the application should be assembled in this order:

- Photocopy of the signed NEH Application Cover Sheet Table of Contents

- One page summary of the project (may be single-spaced)

- Narrative description of the project (double-spaced)

- Project budget (photocopy of the original NEH Budget Form and the budget narrative)

- Appendices:
  Workplans or schedules

  Reading and resource lists, technical specifications, syllabi, if any

  Resumes for all project personnel

  Documentation of the commitment of key project personnel, including those not affiliated with the applicant institution (for example, advisory board members or technical consultants)

# NOTES

**Eligible Gifts and Donors**

Only gifts of money, including the net proceeds from the sale of noncash gifts, that will be used to support budgeted project activities during the grant period are eligible to be matched with federal funds. The source, date of transfer, and amount of the gift or net proceeds from the sale of a noncash gift, must be documented in the applicant's records.

Both restricted gifts (gifts that are given specifically in support of a project) and unrestricted gifts (gifts that may be used at the recipient's discretion) are eligible to be matched if the donors give the gifts directly to the applicant.

If a gift of money is given to an individual or organization associated with the project rather than directly to the applicant, that gift normally will not be deemed eligible to release federal matching funds. The only exception is if the donor has given the gift specifically in support of the project and control over the expenditure of these funds is transferred to the applicant.

Applicants should note that the following items are not eligible to be matched with federal funds: federally appropriated funds, deferred and noncash gifts, income earned from gifts after they are transferred to the applicant, and income received from any fees for participation in project activities.

Ineligible donors include the applicant who will carry out the project and any institutions or individuals who are involved in project activities and who will receive some sort of remuneration from project funds. To avoid any possibility of conflict of interest, a gift should not be used to release federal matching funds when there is the appearance that the donor might benefit in any way by giving a gift to a particular project.

## Presidential Directives

The National Endowment for the Humanities participates in two government-wide Presidential Directives. Executive Order 12876 was promulgated in order to help strengthen and ensure the long-term viability of the nation's Historically Black Colleges and Universities, and Executive Order 12900 was issued by the White House on behalf of education excellence for Hispanic Americans. The NEH encourages applications that respond to these Presidential Directives.

## Non-Profit Tax-Exempt Status

Any private, nonprofit and tax-exempt organization, college or university, or branch of state or local government that is established in the United States may apply. To be eligible to receive NEH funding, applicants must have obtained tax-exempt status by the time funding decisions are made. Accordingly, by accepting a grant, the recipient certifies that it has tax-exempt status. It should be understood by the grant recipient that, in the event an award of a grant is erroneously made to an organization, institution, or group subsequently determined to be ineligible for a grant, the award may be terminated.

## Equal Opportunity Statement

Endowment programs do not discriminate on the basis of race, color, national origin, sex, disability, or age. For further information, write to the Equal Employment Opportunity Officer, National Endowment for the Humanities, 1100 Pennsylvania Avenue, N.W., Washington, D.C. 20506. TDD: (202) 606-8282 (this is a special Telephone Device for the Deaf).

## Compliance with Other Federal Laws

Applicants should be aware that a number of other federal laws and regulations apply to Endowment-supported projects. Depending on the project, these may include compliance with

- the NEH Code of Ethics governing research, publication, and public programming in projects related to American Indian, Aleut, Eskimo, or native Hawaiian peoples;
- Department of Labor minimum compensation requirements;
- a Congressional preference for the purchase of American-made equipment and products.

Other requirements may apply, and applicants are encouraged to consult with Endowment officers early in the application process.

# Analyzing Real Grant Proposals

## Grant #3—Questions

1. What kind of a grant is this; local, state, or federal?

   _____

2. What "missing" parts of this grant would you have if you had written to the National Endowment for the Humanities for a hard copy?

   _____

3. Three types of proposals are sought.  What are they?

   _____

   _____

   _____

4. Briefly, according to what criteria will the proposals be evaluated?

   _____

   _____

   _____

   _____

   _____

5. Which grantees are required to have an audit?

   _____

6. Can you apply by FAX or e-mail?

   _____

7. How many copies of the application itself must be sent in the application package?

   _____

# Analyzing Real Grant Proposal Forms

## Grant #4

If you had seen this one first, you might have quit. It is very long! Look over the materials on the next pages:

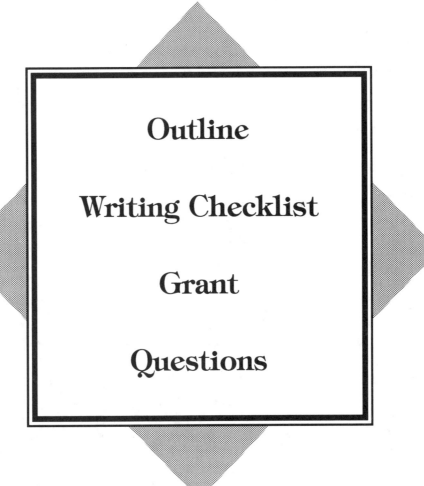

Outline

Writing Checklist

Grant

Questions

Write your answers on the pages or on copies of the pages.

(You could reproduce enough sets for everyone on the grant committee and compare answers.)

### When in Doubt, Call the Funder

If you need more information about anything, call the funder of the grant for clarification. When you come across the funder's information numbers, write them here. Also, note the mailing address.

Telephone number: _____

Fax number: _____

Mailing address: _____

# Analyzing Real Grant Proposals

## Grant #4—Outline

Use the outline below to complete your Writing Checklist (pages 162 and 163) for grant #4.

**Outline**

I.  **Formatting Issues**

   A.  Determine the exact number of pages you must have or are allowed to have. Check:

      1.  Minimum number required (if there is one)

      2.  Maximum number allowed

      3.  Whether or not attachments are allowed

   B.  Check the page layout requirements.

      1.  Width of margins

      2.  Size of font

      3.  Justification

      4.  Spacing of lines

      5.  Numbering of pages

II.  **Required and/or Allowed Elements Which May Include:**

   A.  Title

   B.  Abstract

   C.  Table of Contents

   D.  Introduction

   E.  Goals (vision/mission statement)

   F.  Statement of Needs

   G.  Objectives (stated in measurable terms)

   H.  Activities (how objective will be met)

   I.  Management

   J.  Personnel

   K.  Time Lines

   L.  Resources as Solutions

   M.  Evaluation

   N.  Dissemination

   O.  Budget

   P.  Attachments

# Analyzing Real Grant Proposals

## Grant #4—Writing Checklist

Make photocopies of pages 160–163, and give a set to everyone involved in studying this grant proposal. Ask all of the participants to search the grant for the information listed below. It is important to know the guidelines of a grant so that you can follow them exactly. If the readers (scorers, judges) see that you did not follow the formatting requirements, they may be bound by the rules to throw out your proposal without even reading it.

---

### Formatting Issues

**A. Number of Pages**

1. Minimum number required _____

2. Maximum number allowed _____

3. Attachments allowed (check one)   ❑ Yes   ❑ No

**B. Layout of Pages**

1. Width of margins _____

2. Size of font _____

3. Justification _____

4. Spacing of lines _____

5. Numbering of lines _____

---

# Analyzing Real Grant Proposals

## Grant #4—Writing Checklist *(cont.)*

If an element in this grant is called something else than what is listed, note the term under the column entitled AKA (Also Known As).  You may need to refer to the definitions section of this book to do this.

| Elements | Required | Allowed | AKA |
|---|---|---|---|
| Title | | | |
| Abstract | | | |
| Table of Contents | | | |
| Introduction | | | |
| Goal/Vision/Mission | | | |
| Statement of Needs | | | |
| Objectives | | | |
| Activities | | | |
| Management | | | |
| Personnel | | | |
| Time Lines | | | |
| Resources | | | |
| Evaluation | | | |
| Dissemination | | | |
| Budget | | | |
| Attachments | | | |

(If attachments are allowed, what will they consist of?  Is there anything that you *cannot* attach?) _____

# Guidelines for Preparing Applications, Fiscal Year 1996

# Telecommunications and Information Infrastructure Assistance Program

### National Telecommunications and Information Administration
### U.S. Department of Commerce

## CONTACTING THE TIIAP OFFICE

Information on TIIAP can be obtained by contacting the TIIAP office.

Contact may be made via...

**Mail:**

> U.S. Department of Commerce
> National Telecommunications and Information Administration
> Office of Telecommunications and Information Applications
> TIIAP, Room 4090
> 14th Street and Constitution Avenue, N.W.
> Washington, D.C. 20230

**Telephone:** (202) 482-2048

**Fax:** (202) 501-5136

**E-mail:** tiiap@ntia.doc.gov

**Electronic Information Resources:**

Information about NTIA and TIIAP, including the Guidelines for Preparing Applications and the Notice of Solicitation of Grant Applications, can be retrieved electronically via the Internet through ftp,gopher and the World Wide Web.

To reach the ftp server, ftp to ftp.ntia.doc.gov. Use the login name of **anonymous** and use your e-mail address as the password. Change to the /pub/grantinfo directory to find TIIAP files.

To reach the gopher server, point your gopher client at gopher.ntia.doc.gov and login as gopher.

To reach the TIIAP home page on NTIA's WWW server, use http://www.ntia.doc.gov/tiiap/

**Receiving Information by Automatic Fax Back:**

Information on TIIAP can also be retrieved via an automatic fax back system by calling the TIIAP fax back number: (202) 501-2303. Callers will receive recorded voice instructions for having TIIAP documents faxed automatically to the fax machine of their choice.

# I. HOW TO USE THIS BOOKLET

The *Guidelines for Preparing Applications (Guidelines)* booklet is designed to help applicants prepare a project proposal for the NTIA's Telecommunications and Information Infrastructure Assistance Program (TIIAP) fiscal year 1996 grant round. Each applicant should take the following steps:

First read the fiscal year 1996 TIIAP <u>Notice of Solicitation of Grant Applications</u> *(Notice)*, which must be used in conjunction with the Guidelines. The Notice appears at the beginning of this booklet.

After reviewing the three program categories described in the Notice, decide which category best fits your proposal. The three categories are **Demonstration projects, Access projects, and Planning projects.**

Reread the evaluation criteria in the *Notice*. While the evaluation criteria are equally weighted, **some criteria are qualifying criteria which the projects must satisfy if they are to be evaluated fully. Note that the criteria used to evaluate applications in the three program categories are not identical.**

Read the section "Completing the TIIAP Application" beginning on page two of the *Guidelines*. Note that some instructions in this section apply only to applications in Demonstration projects, while others apply only to applications in Access projects or to applications in Planning projects.

Read the "Application Checklist" on the inside back cover of the *Guidelines* to make sure your application is complete.

This document contains all of the information and Standard Forms needed to submit a TIIAP proposal, including:

- <u>Notice of Solicitation of Grant Applications</u> and the application deadline
- instructions about application format
- instructions for writing the Project Narrative
- instructions for preparing and presenting a Budget Request
- instructions for completing the required Standard Forms
- a table listing the names, addresses, telephone numbers, and fax numbers of the <u>State Single Points of Contact</u>

# II. COMPLETING THE TIIAP APPLICATION

## A. Introduction

This section provides instructions for preparing the TIIAP application. It describes the kinds of information that should be included in a proposal, discusses the mechanics of assembling the application copies, and provides step-by-step instructions for completing the application forms.

## B. Application Deadline

**The deadline time and date for all applications is 5 p.m. EST on Thursday, April 4, 1996. It is your responsibility to ensure that NTIA receives your application before the deadline.**

> ## Applications received after that time and date will not be accepted.

## C. Contacting the TIIAP Office After the Deadline

After the application deadline, no applicant may contact TIIAP program staff to discuss any aspect of an application.

## D. Choosing an Application Area

TIIAP supports projects in the following application areas: <1>

**Community-wide Networking**
**Health**
**Pre-School and K-12 Education**
**Higher Education**
**Library and Lifelong Learning Services**
**Human Services**
**Public Safety**

In order to assign each application to a peer review panel with appropriate expertise, TIIAP requires that each application be identified with one of the seven application areas listed above that best categorizes the project being proposed.

Applicants are asked to choose the application area that best describes the project they propose. This application area is considered the "primary application area." If appropriate, applicants may also identify a second application area that applies to the project. For example, if a project primarily emphasizes community-wide networking but also includes a significant library services component, the primary application area would be "Community-wide Networking" and the secondary application area would be "Library and Lifelong Learning Services."

All proposals must be identified with at least one of the application areas described above. **The responsibility for choosing the application area that best fits the proposed project is the applicant's.**

## E. General Instructions for Preparing Applications

Materials Required for a TIIAP Application. Please assemble the TIIAP application materials in the following order:

- **Standard Form 424**, *Application for Federal Assistance* (see page five of the Guidelines)
- **Project Narrative**—Six (6) pages for Demonstration projects (see page 10); five (5) pages for Access projects
  (see page 16); five (5) pages for Planning projects (see page 21)
- (**Optional:** Appendices to the Project Narrative, such as timelines, diagrams, maps, letters of support, etc.)
- **Standard Form 424A,** *Budget Information—Nonconstruction Programs* (see page 25)
  - ○ Budget Narrative (see page 28)
  - ○ Statement of Matching Funds (see page 36)
- **Standard Forms**
  - ○ 424B, *Assurances* (see page 39)
  - ○ CD-511, *Certifications* (see page 39)
  - ○ LLL, *Disclosure of Lobbying Activities* (if applicable) (see page 39)
  - ○ CD-346, *Applicant for Funding Assistance* (if applicable) (see page 40)

**Completeness of Applications.** A TIIAP application is complete only when it contains the above-referenced items and original signed copies of all of the applicable Standard Forms. The application, including a Project Narrative and other supporting materials, must be complete, legible, and easily understandable.

> **Failure to submit a complete TIIAP application by the application deadline will result in the application being rejected by TIIAP.**

**Pagination.** The pages of a TIIAP application should be numbered consecutively, starting with the first page of the Project Narrative. Please number the Budget Narrative and the Statement of Matching funds as 424A-1, 424A-2, etc. Applicants may insert a Table of Contents after the Standard Form 424 and before the Project Narrative to assist reviewers in locating information in the proposal.

**Page Formats.** The proposal should be typed, single-spaced, on 8 1/2" x 11" paper. All text should be prepared using a font of no less than 12 points with margins of no less than one inch (1").

**Total Number of Copies.** Each applicants must submit one (1) original signed proposal and five (5) copies of the proposal, unless doing so would present a financial hardship, in which case the applicant may submit one (1) original and two (2) copies of the proposal. The original and one (1) copy should be stapled; the other copies should be in looseleaf form.

**Stapled Copies.** The original copy of the proposal should be stapled in the upper left corner. The copy with original signatures should be clearly marked "Original." Each duplicate proposal (see below) should be clearly marked "Copy."

**Looseleaf Copies.** In addition in the two stapled copies each applicant should submit four looseleaf copies of the application. These copies will be used by reviewers. Each of these copies should be legible and clipped with a binder clip. **Note: please do not include copies of Standard Forms 424B, CD-511, LLL, or CD-346 in these looseleaf copies.**

**Signatures.** Signatures are required in the following places in the application:

- bottom (box 18d) of **Standard Form 424**, *Application for Federal Assistance*
- back page of **Standard Form 424B**, *Assurances*
- bottom of back page of **Standard Form CD-511**, *Certifications*
- bottom of **Standard Form LLL**, *Disclosure of Lobbying Activities* (if applicable, see page 39 of the *Guidelines*)
- bottom of **Standard Form CD-346**, *Applicant for Funding Assistance* for each individual (if applicable, see page 40)

Standard Forms 424, 424B, CD-511, and LLL should be signed by someone who is authorized to commit the applicant organization, such as the Chief Executive Officer, Chief Financial Officer, President, or Executive Director. Original signatures should be in blue ink so that the original proposal can be easily distinguished from proposal copies.

**Page Limit.** Forty pages, including all text, tables, illustrations, maps, letters, references, resumes, and supporting documents, excluding the Standard Forms and all budget information. Quality, not quantity, is what counts! Pages can be saved by following the suggestions below.

- Do not include supplemental material not specifically requested in the Guidelines, either bound with the proposal or separately bound.
- Do not include company sales catalogs, annual reports, or video or audio tapes.

**Amendments to Applications.** Amendments to an application may not be submitted after the application deadline unless specifically requested by the TIIAP staff. TIIAP will notify applicants if any additional information is needed to evaluate the application properly. Information may be requested of applicants at any time.

**Changes in Contact Information.** If the contact information submitted in Box 5 of Standard Form 424 changes after the proposal has been submitted, the applicant should immediately notify TIIAP in writing.

## F. Instructions for Completing Standard Form 424, *Application for Federal Assistance*

**Required for All Applicants**

Standard Form 424 is required by the Office of Management and Budget as a face sheet to all applications for federal assistance. It asks for information about your organization and your project.

**Here are box-by-box instructions about how to fill out Standard Form 424.**

**Box 2:** Enter the date on which the proposal is being submitted.

**Boxes 3, 4:** Please leave blank.

**Box 5:** In the section labeled "Legal Name," enter the legal name of the organization that is applying for a grant. Do not enter the legal name of the individual who is applying on behalf of the organization.

In the section labeled "Organizational Unit," enter the name of the department, division, or other organizational unit that will perform the proposed project. For example, the legal name may be the "ABC County Hospital," and the organizational unit may be the "Department of Information Services."

In the section labeled "Address," please enter a street address, not a post office box number. Also, please remember to include the name of the county; this is used for administrative purposes.

In the section labeled "Name and Telephone," please include a fax number and an electronic mail address, if available, of the contact person.

**Box 6:** The Employer Identification Number (EIN) is assigned by the Internal Revenue Service. Every employer should have one.

**Box 7:** Enter the most appropriate letter in the box. If you are a non-profit organization to which none of the labels applies, please enter "N" for "Other" and type in "Non-profit." Please note that individuals and for-profit organizations are not eligible to apply.

**Box 11:** On the first line of this box, enter the category of the application (i.e., "Demonstration" or "Access" or "Planning"). On the second line of this box, enter the primary application area (an acceptable entry must be one of the seven application areas, exactly as listed on page 2 of the Guidelines.) Starting on the third line of this box, enter a descriptive title of the project. Do not enter a summary of the project.

**Box 12:** List the cities and/or counties affected by the project. If a project is statewide or involves multiple states, please list only the states. If a project is nationwide in scope, please enter "nationwide."

**Box 13:** In the section labeled "Start Date," enter the date on which the project will begin. Note that the project may begin at anytime after the application deadline, but applicants should read the caution about premature obligation of funds. Please enter a full date, such as, "8/1/96."

In the section labeled "End Date," enter the date on which the project will terminate. For applications in Demonstration projects, this date may not be more than 24 months from the date entered as the start date. For applications in Access projects, this date may not be more than 18 months from the date entered as the start date. For applications in Planning projects, this date may not be more than 12 months from the date entered as the start date.

**Box 14:** In the section labeled "Applicant," enter the state and district number, e.g., "Nebraska-2." **Do not** enter the name of the Congressional representative. **Only one district** should be listed; it should correspond to the address of the applicant listed in Box 5.

In the section labeled "Project," enter the state (or states) and the Congressional district (or districts) that will be directly affected by the project.

**Box 15a:** Enter the funding request from NTIA for the entire duration of the project. Remember that Demonstration projects are limited to 24 months, Access projects are limited to 18 months, and Planning projects are limited to 12 months.

**Box 15b:** Enter the estimated funding (both cash and in-kind contributions) to be provided by the applicant.

**Box 15c:** Enter the estimated funding (both cash and in-kind contributions) to be provided by a state government or governments. If the applicant is a state government entity, enter the estimated funding in Box 15b as an applicant contribution, and leave this box blank.

**Box 15d:** Enter the estimated funding (both cash and in-kind contributions) to be provided by a local government of governments. If the applicant is a local government entity, enter the estimated funding in Box 15b as an applicant contribution, and leave this box blank.

**Box 15e:** Enter the estimated funding (both cash and in-kind contributions) to be provided by other sources (e.g., foundations, private sector contributors).

**Box 15f:** Leave blank.

**Box 15g:** Enter the total of Boxes 15a-15e.

**Box 16:** TIIAP is covered by <u>Executive Order 12372</u>. All applicants are required to submit a copy of their application to their state <u>Single Point of Contact</u> (SPOC) (see names and addresses of state SPOC offices beginning on page 41) for review, with the exception of applicants from the following states, which do not have SPOC offices:

| | | | |
|---|---|---|---|
| Alaska | Kansas | Nebraska | Tennessee |
| Colorado | Louisiana | Oklahoma | Virginia |
| Connecticut | Massachusetts | Oregon | Washington |
| Hawaii | Minnesota | Pennsylvania | |
| Idaho | Montana | South Dakota | |

Applicants should indicate the date on which a copy of the proposal was submitted to the state SPOC office. If the application is from a state listed above or a state has for some reason declined to review the proposal, check the box next to "or program has not been selected by state for review." **Do not** check the box next to "program is not covered by E.O. 12372."

**Box 17:** Unless your organization is delinquent on a federal debt, **be sure** to check "No." If your organization is delinquent on a Federal debt, explain the circumstances on a separate sheet attached to this form.

**Box 18:** Enter the name, title and telephone number of someone who is authorized to commit the applicant organization. Have the authorized representative sign the form in blue ink so that the original signature can be distinguished from the copies. Do not forget to date the signature.

## G. Instructions for Preparing Project Narrative

### Required for all applicants

The **Project Narrative** explains what you plan to do and why your project should be supported by NTIA. It is your opportunity to make a clear and convincing presentation of the goals of your project and the means with which you expect to achieve these goals, to independent reviewers, the TIIAP staff, and the selecting official at NTIA. Each of these readers needs to understand quickly and easily what you are proposing and how well your proposal responds to the evaluation criteria published in the <u>Notice</u>. Further, your narrative must show how you will carry out your project within the resources, such as personnel, time, and equipment, you have allocated.

In preparing the Project Narrative, be specific and do not assume that reviewers will be familiar either with your organization or with the details of the issues you raise. Reviewers will base their evaluation on the material contained in the proposals.

### Project Categories

The Fiscal Year 1996 TIIAP grant program is divided into three categories: **Demonstration** projects, **Access** projects, and **Planning** projects. NTIA will award approximately sixty-five percent (65%) of the funds to support Demonstration projects, approximately thirty percent (30%) of the funds to support Access projects, and approximately five percent (5%) of the funds to support Planning projects, unless the quality and/or number of submissions in one of these categories does not, in NTIA's judgement, merit the proposed allocation of funds.

The primary goal of **Demonstration** projects is to demonstrate new, high-impact, useful applications of information infrastructure which hold significant potential for replication in other communities. The projects must deploy, use, and evaluate innovative applications of information infrastructure to address a particular problem or set of problems in real-world environments. Projects selected in this category will have a high potential to serve as models for other communities and to demonstrate results within the grant period. No award in the Demonstration projects will exceed $750,000.

The primary goal of **Access** projects is to provide underserved communities, populations, or geographic areas with greater access to the benefits of the National Information Infrastructure (NII). Access projects emphasize serving groups of people who have not been adequately served in the past, and increasing their access to services and information. Access projects place a greater emphasis on reducing disparities than on innovation. Hence, an Access project may build on or emulate a successful model which has gained widespread acceptance in the field. No award in the Access projects category will exceed $250,000.

The primary goal of **Planning** projects is to enable organizations, or groups of organizations, to develop strategies for the enhanced application of information infrastructure. Planning projects provide opportunities to bring coalitions together to form firm foundations on which to implement information infrastructure equitably, to examine opportunities that investment in information infrastructure creates, to aggregate demand for telecommunications services among multiple organizations, and to understand the needs of potential end users. Planning projects are encouraged for rural or underserved populations where an enhanced telecommunications infrastructure could provide greater economic opportunity. The end result of a planning project should be a credible plan for deploying and using information infrastructure and sufficient support from the community to implement the plan. No award in the Planning projects category will exceed $100,000.

Each of the categories is described in greater detail in the Notice of Solicitation of Grant Applications.

---

**Because the evaluation criteria for Demonstration projects, for Access projects, and for Planning projects are not identical, applicants in each category have different sets of instructions for preparing the Project Narrative. The following are instructions for applicants for Demonstration project grants.**

**Applicants in the Access category should go to page 16 of the Guidelines.**
**Applicants in the Planning category should go to page 21 of the Guidelines.**

---

## INSTRUCTIONS FOR DEMONSTRATION PROJECT APPLICANTS

The Demonstration Project Narrative must contain an Executive Summary and must address each of the evaluation criteria listed in the Notice of Solicitation of Grant Applications that apply to Demonstration projects: Problem Definition; Technical Approach; Ability to Serve as a Model; Applicant Qualifications; Partnerships and Community Support; Support for End Users; Evaluation and Dissemination; and Reducing Disparities in Access to and Use of the NII. Budget is a separate component and is described on page 24 of the Guidelines. The Project Narrative must not exceed six single-spaced pages. **Proposals whose narrative exceed this limit will not be considered by TIIAP.** Note that the sections of the Project Narrative that follow the Executive Summary correspond to the evaluation criteria listed in the Notice.

## EXECUTIVE SUMMARY

Every proposal needs to begin with an Executive Summary. Give a concise Executive Summary of the project which does not exceed 125 words. Begin the Executive Summary with the following sentence: "This is a Demonstration project intended for the (choose one of the seven application areas listed on page 2 of the *Guidelines*) primary application area and (if applicable) for the (choose another one of the application areas listed on page 2 of the *Guidelines*) secondary application area."

(For example, you might begin the Executive Summary with this sentence: "This is a Demonstration project intended for the Human Services primary application area.") The Executive Summary should briefly cover the core aspects of the project: the goal(s) of the project; the community or communities to be served; the organizations participating as project partners; and the technologies to be employed. The Executive Summary should be factual rather than rhetorical in nature. **It is likely that, if the project is recommended for support, the Executive Summary will be incorporated into TIIAP publications and announcements.**

## Problem Definition

> **Demonstration projects will be evaluated against nine criteria. While each criterion is weighted equally, the following criterion is one of the three qualifying criteria: Problem Definition, Technical Approach, and Ability to Serve as a Model. Demonstration project applicants must fully meet each qualifying criterion. If an application is deemed inadequate on any one of these, it will not be further evaluated.**

Applicants must **clearly** link their proposed technology projects to a specific problem or problems in one of the seven application areas. The need(s) or problem(s) to be addressed should be thoroughly documented, using comparative data such as statistics. Applicants must explain how the use of technology will contribute to the solution of the problem(s) they define, and they must relate the solution to clear and measurable **outcomes** or results. The scope of the project must meet TIIAP eligibility criteria (see the "Eligibility" section on page three of the *Notice*).

Since you must adhere to rigorous page and space limitations, **the problem definition must be specific and convincing.** Do not substitute rhetoric for a cogent and systematic presentation.

Applicants must present a clear and convincing link between the project they propose and the benefits they expect to achieve. Statements such as "our schools lack access to the information highway, and this project will connect them to it" do not provide an acceptable definition of the problem, particularly in the Demonstration project category. You must specify the problem to be addressed in as much detail as needed (for example, "doctors in this rural area do not have timely access to the newest treatment protocols, and it is difficult for them to maintain their skills levels when the nearest major medical center is five hours away by car") and describe the outcomes you expect from your project (for example, "doctors and other medical personnel will interact with distant specialists more frequently to seek confirmation of diagnoses or additional suggestions for treatment, leading to improved patient care, as measured by a reduction in the number of repeat visits for the same illness and a higher expressed rate of patient satisfaction").

Note that quantification and measurement of outcomes are essential to understanding whether the project is effective or not. However, measurements, such as "more users have logged on in this quarter than the last," are not necessarily useful in **qualitative** terms. Is the increase in usage sustained? How are the services being used? Can improvements in motivation, behavior, or results be attributed to the increased numbers of log-ons, or the increased time on-line? More users logging on, only to give up in frustration after a single session, is an indicator of trouble, not success. Please remember this when preparing the section on "Evaluation and Dissemination."

---

**Demonstration projects will be evaluated against nine criteria. While each criterion is weighted equally, the following criterion is one of the three qualifying criteria: Problem Definition, Technical Approach, and Ability to Serve as a Model. Demonstration project applicants must fully meet each qualifying criterion. If an application is deemed inadequate on any one of these, it will not be further evaluated.**

---

TIIAP defines technical quality as the application of appropriate information technology consistent with the vision of a nationwide, seamless, interactive network of networks, not as innovation for its own sake. Use this section to describe in detail the technology that you will employ in the project, the rationale for employing that particular technology, and how it will be organized. Reviewers will scrutinize this section to determine how well what you are actually planning to do supports the goals set forth in the section on "Problem Definition." It is very important for you to be concrete and specific in this section. There should be no confusion among the reviewers as to what the technology will do and how it will work.

Provide an overview of the system to be deployed and discuss in specific terms the equipment, software, and network services that you will use. You are encouraged to append a network diagram which shows the major equipment items, information services to be utilized, their locations, and the connections among them.

If you are installing computers, identify the type of computer and operating systems (e.g., Macintosh Power PC 8100, Pentium 90 with Windows 95), how many will be installed and where they will be located. For network connections, identify the methods (e.g., each computer will be connected to a regional server through dialup lines with 14.4 Kbps modems, each site will have a T1 speed access line to a switched ATM network service). Identify software packages that will be employed and any information or communication protocols or standards that you will use (e.g., HL7 for medical information, Z39.50 for libraries).

In addition to describing the technical plans, you will need to address four issues: interoperability, scalability, maintenance/upgrading of the system, and privacy.

1. You must show how the system that you will deploy will or could **interoperate** with other relevant networks or services. For example, if you are planning to deploy a network that would be used to transmit medical images among several institutions, you should describe how your network would or could be integrated with other information systems at those institutions or elsewhere in the community. You should also discuss your use of industry standards and, if you have chosen any proprietary solutions where standards are available, you should provide justification.

2. You must address the issue of **scalability** by discussing how the system you intend to deploy can accommodate growth beyond the scale defined for the grant period. This growth could be a growth in the number of users within the community, a growth in the geographic area to be served, or a growth in the services that would be offered with the system (i.e., discuss the capability to add services to those that will be provided initially).

3. You must describe your plans for **maintaining the system** you deploy and for upgrading the technology, if applicable, to exploit new opportunities made possible by advances in technology.

4. You must discuss your plans for protecting the **privacy of end users** and individuals affected by the system and for avoiding the disclosure of confidential information. If you believe that privacy and confidentiality are not important issues in your project, you must state so clearly and discuss your reasoning. If your project will involve the storage or usage of confidential information, such as student grades or medical records, you must describe in detail both the technological mechanisms you will employ to maintain system security and unauthorized access to information and the policy mechanisms (e.g., staff education, usage guidelines) you will develop to deter improper use.

This section must also include a discussion of the project implementation schedule. Include specific tasks, milestones, and dates in this discussion. Charts or tables containing this information can be appended after the narrative and are very helpful in presenting timetables in a clear and organized manner.

**Ability to Serve as a Model**

> **Demonstration projects will be evaluated against nine criteria. While each criterion is weighted equally, the following criterion is one of the three qualifying criteria: Problem Definition, Technical Approach, and Ability to Serve as a Model. Demonstration project applicants must fully meet each qualifying criterion. If an application is deemed inadequate on any one of these, it will not be further evaluated.**

This section is your opportunity to explain the significance of your project in a national context. For Demonstration projects, it is not enough to show that the project will have substantial benefit in your community, you must demonstrate the potential value of your project to communities across the nation. Start this section by identifying the model itself as clearly as possible. (For example, the model is "the use of electronic mail and discussion groups to provide peer support to homebound persons with disabilities in rural areas.") Discuss what about your project and the model it proposes is unusual or innovative and make specific reference to other activities and projects in your field. Explain what this project will add to what is already known about using information infrastructure in addressing the problems your project will attempt to solve. Reviewers will be instructed to look for evidence in your proposal that you have examined other, similar projects and are familiar with their results. If your project will duplicate or repeat elements of another project, you should be clear about how your project will differ and what it is expected to add.

Once you have established the innovative nature of the model, you should address the potential impact of the project and the potential for the model to be replicated in other communities.

Is the problem you are addressing common to many communities? What about your model is generalizable? Can you provide evidence that the model you intend to demonstrate is of interest to other communities? (Letters of support from persons not directly involved with your project may be helpful in supporting this point.)

In addition, the program will examine whether a subsequent evaluation of the project can contribute significantly to our understanding of how the NII can be used to improve the delivery of a wide range of social services and promote economic development.

You should also, in discussing the potential replicability of the model, discuss its long-term financial viability. Because TIIAP expects Demonstration projects to be innovative, the approaches demonstrated may not always be immediately cost-effective. However, for any model to be useful, it should demonstrate reasonable potential for sustainability without continuing federal support.

## Applicant Qualifications

Use this section to describe the qualifications of the participating institutions, the key personnel associated with the project, their relationship to the applicant organization, and the applicant's experience in addressing information-related issues. Experience may be demonstrated in a variety of ways, including projects successfully completed and participation in comprehensive planning activities. This does not mean that all applicants must have successfully completed projects similar to, or identical to, the project being proposed; nor does it require that all key personnel must already be employed by one of the participating organizations. The applicant may propose hiring, or contracting with, individuals possessing the relevant expertise. In these instances, however, it is imperative that the proposal describe in detail the qualifications of individuals who would be hired or contracted with during the project award period. If specific individuals have not yet been selected to hold key positions in the project, you should provide brief position descriptions and discussions of expected qualifications for those positions. In addition, each applicant should present evidence that it is not only a capable organization, but that it is an appropriate and credible organization to undertake the project it proposes.

## Partnerships and Community Support

Proposals must provide evidence of public and private sector support and involvement. The extent to which applicants have included diverse sectors of the community in project design and development will be considered an integral part of the proposal. A proposal should present a clear discussion of who the partners will be, what their respective roles in the project will be, what benefits each expects to receive, and what each partner will apply to the project in the form of cash contributions, personnel, or other resources. In addition to identifying and describing project partners, an applicant must provide documentation of the partners' commitment to the project, such as letters from the partners to the applicant describing their roles and contributions. If you have worked with these partners on projects in the past, discuss the nature and results of those projects and the project responsibilities assumed by each collaborator.

## Support for End Users

Expanding upon the problem definition, you should provide a precise definition of the end user population to be served. Demographic or other relevant statistical information on the end user population should be included. Discuss the steps you have taken to assess end user needs and demand for the services you intend to provide. The proposal should describe strategies for addressing end user needs, and cultivating or increasing their skills.

This section should also explain clearly how targeted end users will employ the services to be offered. It should also be clear how they will benefit from the services offered. Finally, you should document end user involvement in the design and planning of the project. One or more specific scenarios of end user interaction with the technology would be extremely useful here. For example, the following scenario is excerpted from a successful TIIAP application: "An elderly patient arrives at the emergency room complaining of a chronic cough. A message is sent over the network to the city department of health, reporting that a likely case of tuberculosis has been found. The physician directs the department electronically to arrange for the patient to be followed by the department for Directly Observed Therapy. Later, a visiting nurse uses a hand-held computer to report on the patient's condition."

## Evaluation and Dissemination

The evaluation plan that you present should refer to the goals and outcomes described in **Section 1 (Problem Definition)**, describe what indicators you will use to determine the success of the project, and tell how you will measure them. Be careful to distinguish how you will monitor the progress of the project against the time line provided in **Section 2, (Technical Approach)** (e.g., have all the milestones been met?), from how you will evaluate the usage of the technology you will deploy (e.g., how many users use the system each week and for what do they use it?), from how you will evaluate the outcomes to be affected by the project (e.g., have childhood immunization rates increased?). Plans for outcome evaluations should also include the capability of documenting and analyzing unexpected outcomes. In presenting your plans, be sure to discuss the evaluation tools (e.g., on-line surveys, focus groups) you intend to employ. You must also identify the people who will be responsible for conducting the evaluation and describe their qualifications if you have not already done so in the section on "Applicant Qualifications."

This section must also include a presentation of your plans for disseminating information about your project and the lessons that you learn. Be as specific as possible—if you are planning on presenting at conferences, identify the conferences; if you plan to publish articles on the project, identify the journals to which you intend to submit papers.

Please note that evaluating the impact of your project is not the same as monitoring the progress of the project relative to the timeline you have proposed in **Section 2, (Technical Approach).** Moreover, merely quantifying the use of the systems you propose, without performing a qualitative assessment of that use, is not an acceptable evaluation strategy.

Effective evaluation includes:

- a clear statement of the problem(s) you will address
- a clear description of the relationship between the use of technology and improvements you expect to see in outcomes or results, relative to the problems you have described

**Reducing Disparities in Access to and Use of the NII**

In this section, you should identify the existing disparities in access, using specific supporting quantitative and/or demographic data, and describe the barriers to access that cause the disparity. Barriers to access may be geographic, linguistic, cultural, physical, or economic in nature.

Include in this section a profile of the community or communities to be served and the intended beneficiaries of the project. In this profile, cite supporting statistics (e.g., per capita income, percent of households living in poverty, population density, size of the region, etc.), as appropriate. In addition, maps or other geographical representations of the project's impact may be useful in describing the project.

Finally, you should describe the specific steps which you will use to accommodate the particular conditions in the community and to overcome the specific barriers to access or use of the NII that the community faces.

---

**Applicants in the Demonstration category should turn to page 24 in the Guidelines and read "Instructions for Preparing a Budget Request."**

---

## INSTRUCTIONS FOR ACCESS PROJECT APPLICANTS

The Access Project Narrative must contain an Executive Summary and must address each of the evaluation criteria listed in the Notice of Solicitation of Grant Applications that apply to Access projects: Problem Definition; Reducing Disparities in Access to and Use of the NII; Technical Approach; Applicant Qualifications; Partnerships and Community Support; Support for End Users; Evaluation and Dissemination; and Sustainability. Budget is a separate component and is discussed on page 24 of the *Guidelines*. The Project Narrative must not exceed five single-spaced pages. **Proposals whose narratives exceed this limit will not be considered by TIIAP.** Note that the sections of the Project Narrative that follow the Executive Summary correspond to the evaluation criteria listed in the Notice.

### EXECUTIVE SUMMARY

Every proposal needs to begin with an Executive Summary. Give a concise Executive Summary of the project which does not exceed 125 words. Begin the Executive Summary with the following sentence: "This is an Access project intended for the (choose one of the seven application areas listed on page 2 of the *Guidelines*) primary application area and, if applicable, for the (choose another one of the seven application areas listed on page 2 of the *Guidelines*) secondary application area." (For example, you might begin the Executive Summary with this sentence: "This is an Access project intended for the Human Services primary application area.") The Executive Summary should briefly cover the core aspects of the project: the goal(s) of the project; the community or communities to be served; the organizations participating as project partners; and the technologies to be employed.

The Executive Summary should be factual rather than rhetorical in nature. **It is likely that, if the project is recommended for support, the Executive Summary will be incorporated into TIIAP publications and announcements.**

**Problem Definition**

> **Access projects will be evaluated against nine criteria. While each criterion is weighted equally, the following criterion is one of the two qualifying criteria: Problem Definition and Reducing Disparities in Access to and Use of the NII. Access project applicants must fully meet both qualifying criteria. If an application is deemed inadequate on either of them, it will not be further evaluated.**

Applicants must **clearly** link their proposed technology projects to a specific problem or problems in one of the seven application areas. The need(s) or problem(s) to be addressed should be thoroughly documented, using comparative data such as statistics. Applicants must explain how the use of technology will contribute to the solution of the problem(s) they define, and they must relate the solution to clear and measurable outcomes or results. The scope of the project must meet TIIAP eligibility criteria (see the "Eligibility" section in the *Notice*).

Since you must adhere to rigorous page and space limitations, **the problem definition must be specific and convincing.** Do not substitute rhetoric for a cogent and systematic presentation.

Applicants often fail to present a clear and convincing link between the project they propose and the benefits they expect to achieve. Statements such as "our schools lack access to the information highway, and this project will connect them to it" do not provide an acceptable definition of the problem. You must specify the problem to be addressed in as much detail as needed (for example, "doctors in this rural area do not have timely access to the newest treatment protocols, and it is difficult for them to maintain their skills levels when the nearest major medical center is five hours away by car") and describe the outcomes you expect from your project (for example, "doctors and other medical personnel will interact with distant specialists more frequently to seek confirmation of diagnoses or additional suggestions for treatment, leading to improved patient care, as measured by a reduction in the number of repeat visits for the same illness and a higher expressed rate of patient satisfaction").

Note that quantification and measurement of outcomes are essential to understanding whether the project is effective or not. However, measurements such as "more users have logged on in this quarter than the last" are not necessarily useful in **qualitative** terms. Is the increase in usage sustained? How are the services being used? Can improvements in motivation, behavior, or results be attributed to the increased numbers of log-ons, or the increased time on-line? More behavior, or users logging on, only to give up in frustration after a single session, is an indicator of trouble, not success. Please remember this when preparing the section on "Evaluation and Dissemination."

---

**Access projects will be evaluated against nine criteria. While each criterion is weighted equally, the following criterion is one of the two qualifying criteria:Problem Definition and Reducing Disparities in Access to and Use of the NII. Access project applicants must fully meet both qualifying criteria. If an application is deemed inadequate on either of them, it will not be further evaluated.**

---

In this section, you should identify the existing disparities in access, using specific supporting quantitative and/or demographic data, and describe the barriers to access that cause the disparities. Barriers to access may be geographic, linguistic, cultural, physical, or economic in nature.

Include in this section a profile of the community or communities to be served and the intended beneficiaries of the project. In this profile, cite supporting statistics (e.g., per capita income, percent of household living in poverty, population density, size of the region, etc.), as appropriate. In addition, maps or other geographical representations of the project's impact may be useful in describing the project.

Finally, you should describe the specific steps which you will use to accommodate the particular conditions in the community and to overcome the specific barriers to access or use of the NII that the community faces.

## Technical Approach

TIIAP defines technical quality as the application of appropriate information technology that is consistent with the vision of a nationwide, seamless, interactive network of networks, not as innovation for its own sake. Use this section to describe in detail the technology that you will employ in the project, the rationale for employing that particular technology, and how it will be organized. Reviewers will scrutinize this section to determine how well what you are actually planning to do supports the goals set forth in the section on "Problem Definition." It is very important for you to be concrete and specific in this section. There should be no confusion among the reviewers as to what the technology will do and how it will work.

Provide an overview of the system to be deployed and discuss in specific terms the equipment, software, and network services that you will use. You are encouraged to append a network diagram which shows the major equipment items, information services to be utilized, their locations, and the connections among them.

If you are installing computers, identify the type of computer and operating system (e.g., Macintosh Power PC 8100, Pentium 90 with Windows 95), how many will be installed and where they will be located. For network connections, identify the methods (e.g., each computer will be connected to a regional server through dial-up lines with 14.4. Kbps modems, each site will have a T1 speed access line to a switched ATM network service). Identify software packages that will be employed and any information or communication protocols or standards that you will use (e.g., HL7 for medical information, Z39.50 for libraries).

In addition to describing the technical plans, you will need to address four issues: interoperability, scalability, maintenance/upgrading of the system, and privacy.

1. You must show how the system that you will deploy will or could **interoperate** with other relevant networks or services. For example, if you are planning to deploy a network that would be used to transmit medical images among several institutions, you should describe how your network would or could be integrated with other information systems at those institutions or elsewhere in the community. You should also discuss your use of industry standards and, if you have chosen any proprietary solutions where standards are available, you should provide justification.

2. You must address the issue of **scalability** by discussing how the system you intend to deploy can accommodate growth beyond the scale defined for the grant period. This growth could be a growth in the number of users within the community, a growth in the geographic area to be served, or a growth in the services that would be offered with the system (i.e., discuss the capability to add services to those that will be provided initially).

3. You must describe your plans for **maintaining the system** you deploy and for upgrading the technology, if applicable, to exploit new opportunities made possible by advances in technology.

4. You must discuss your plans for protecting the **privacy of end users** and individuals affected by the system and for avoiding the disclosure of confidential information. If you believe that privacy and confidentiality are not important issues in your project, you must state so clearly and discuss your reasoning. If your project will involve the storage or usage of confidential information, such as student grades or medical records, you must describe in detail both the technological mechanisms you will employ to maintain system security and unauthorized access to information and the policy mechanisms (e.g., staff education, usage guidelines) you will develop to deter improper use.

This section must also include a discussion of the project implementation schedule. Include specific tasks, milestones, and dates in this discussion. Charts or tables containing this information can be appended after the narrative and are very helpful in presenting timetables in a clear and organized manner.

## Applicant Qualifications

Use this section to describe the qualifications of the participating institutions, the key personnel associated with the project, their relationship to the applicant organization, and the applicant's experience in addressing information-related issues. Experience may be demonstrated in a variety of ways, including projects successfully completed and participation in comprehensive planning activities. This does not mean that all applicants must have successfully completed projects similar to, or identical to, the project being proposed; nor does it require that all key personnel must already be employed by one of the participating organizations.

The applicant may propose hiring, or contracting with, individuals possessing the relevant expertise. In these instances, however, it is imperative that the proposal describe in detail the qualifications of individuals who would be hired or contracted with during the project award period. If specific individuals have not yet been selected to hold key positions in the project, you should provide brief position descriptions and discussions of expected qualifications for those positions.

In addition, each applicant should present evidence that it is not only a capable organization, but that it is an appropriate and credible organization to undertake the project it proposes.

## Partnerships and Community Support

Proposals must provide evidence of public and private sector support and involvement. The extent to which applicants have included diverse sectors of the community in project design and development will be considered an integral part of the proposal. A proposal should present a clear discussion of who the partners will be, what their respective roles in the project will be, what benefits each expects to receive, and what each partner will apply to the project in the form of cash contributions, personnel, or other resources. In addition to identifying and describing project partners, an applicant must provide documentation of the partners' commitment to the project, such as letters from the partners to the applicant describing their roles and contributions. If you have worked with these partners on projects in the past, discuss the nature and results of those projects and the project responsibilities assumed by each collaborator.

## Support for End Users

Expanding upon the problem definition, you should provide a precise definition of the end user population to be served. Demographic or other relevant statistical information on the end user population should be included. Discuss the steps you have taken to assess end user needs and demand for the services you intend to provide. The proposal should describe strategies for addressing end user needs, and cultivating or increasing their skills.

This section should also explain clearly how targeted end users will employ the services to be offered. It should also be clear how they will benefit from the services offered. Finally, you should document end user involvement in the design and planning of the project. One or more specific scenarios of end user interaction with the technology would be extremely useful here. For example, the following scenario is excerpted from a successful TIIAP application: "An elderly patient arrives at the emergency room complaining of a chronic cough. A message is sent over the network to the city department of health, reporting that a likely case of tuberculosis has been found. The physician directs the department electronically to arrange for the patient to be followed by the department for Directly Observed Therapy. Later, a visiting nurse uses a hand-held computer to report on the patient's condition."

## Evaluation and Dissemination

The evaluation plan that you present should refer to the goals and outcomes described in **Section 1, (Problem Definition)**, describe what indicators you will use to determine the success of the project, and tell how you will measure them. Be careful to distinguish how you will monitor the progress of the project against the time line provided in **Section 3 (Technical Approach)** (e.g. have all the milestones been met?), from how you will evaluate the usage of the technology you will deploy (e.g., how many users use the system each week and for what do they use it?), from how you will evaluate the outcomes to be affected by the project (e.g., have childhood immunization rates increased?). Plans for outcome evaluations should also include the capability of documenting and analyzing unexpected outcomes. In presenting your plans, be sure to discuss the evaluation tools (e.g., on-line surveys, focus groups) you intend to employ. You must also identify the people who will be responsible for conducting the evaluation and describe their qualifications if you have not already done so in the section on "Applicant Qualification."

This section must also include a presentation of your plans for disseminating information about your project and the lessons that you learn. Be as specific as possible if you are planning on presenting at conferences, identify the conferences; if you plan to publish articles on the project, identify the journals to which you intend to submit papers.

Please note that evaluating the impact of your project is not the same as monitoring the progress of the project relative to the timeline you have proposed in **Section 3 (Technical Approach).** Moreover, merely quantifying the use of the systems you propose, without performing a qualitative assessment of that use, is not an acceptable evaluation strategy.

## Effective evaluation includes:

- a clear statement of the problem(s) you will address
- a clear description of the relationship between the use of technology and improvements you expect to see in outcomes or results, relative to the problems you have described.

## Sustainability

The applicant must clearly describe a credible plan for sustaining the project economically and operationally beyond the period of federal funding. Regarding economic sustainability, the plan should include discussion of anticipated ongoing expenses and potential sources of revenue. Mechanisms such as membership or user fees should be described, if applicable.

Regarding operational sustainability, the plan should include a discussion of how the project will be managed and operated after the federal funding period ends. The applicant should address whether the start-up partners and their responsibilities for various segments of the project are expected to remain the same or to change over time.

---

**Applicants in the Access project category should turn to page 24 in the Guidelines and read "Instructions for Preparing a Budget Request."**

---

## INSTRUCTIONS FOR PLANNING PROJECT APPLICANTS

The Planning Project Narrative must contain an Executive Summary and must address each of the evaluation criteria listed in the Notice of Solicitation of Grant Applications that apply to Planning projects: Problem Definition; Partnership and Community Support; Reducing Disparities in Access to and Use of the NII; Applicant Qualifications; Support for End Users; and Evaluation and Dissemination. Budget is a separate component and is discussed on page 24 of the Guidelines. The Project Narrative must not exceed five (5) single-spaced pages. Proposals whose narratives exceed this limit will not be considered by TIIAP. Note that the sections of the Project Narrative that follow the Executive Summary correspond to the evaluation criteria listed in the Notice.

## EXECUTIVE SUMMARY

Every proposal needs to begin with an Executive Summary. Give a concise Executive Summary of the project which does not exceed 125 words. Begin the Executive Summary with the following sentence: "This is a Planning project intended for the (choose one of the seven application areas listed on page two of the Guidelines) primary application area and, if applicable, for the (choose another one of the seven application areas listed on page two of the Guidelines) secondary application area." (For example, you might begin the Executive Summary with this sentence: "This is a Planning project intended for the Human Services primary application area.") The Executive Summary should briefly cover the core aspects of the project: the goal(s) of the project; the community or communities to be served; and the organizations participating as project partners. The Executive Summary should be factual rather than rhetorical in nature. **It is likely that, if the project is recommended for support, the Executive Summary will be incorporated into TIIAP publications and announcements.**

### Problem Definition

---

**Planning projects will be evaluated against seven criteria. While each criterion is weighted equally, the following criterion is one of the two qualifying criteria:Problem Definition and Partnerships and Community Support. Planning project applicants must fully meet each qualifying criterion. If an application is deemed inadequate on either of these, it will not be further evaluated.**

---

Applicants must **clearly** link their proposed planning projects to a specific problem or problems in pre-school or K-12 education, health, or another application area.

The need(s) or problem(s) to be addressed should be thoroughly documented, using comparative data such as quantitative statistics. Applicants must explain how the use of technology will contribute to the solution of the problem(s) they define, and they must relate the solution to clear and measurable outcomes or results. The scope of the project must meet TIIAP eligibility criteria (see the "Eligibility" section in the Notice).

Since you must adhere to rigorous page and space limitations, **the problem definition must be specific and convincing.** Do not substitute rhetoric for a cogent and systematic presentation.

Applicants often fail to present a clear and convincing link between the project they propose and the benefits they expect to achieve. Statements such as "our schools lack access to the information highway, and this project will yield a plan to connect them to it" do not provide an acceptable definition of the problem. You must specify the problem to be addressed in as much detail as needed. For example: "The challenges to effective citizen participation in the NII in our region are manifold: the four million citizens in the three counties participating in this project reflect one of the most diverse ethnic, economic, age, and cultural mixes in the country. Connectivity among established institutions, such as libraries and colleges, is in process; however, this process of connectivity has not reached other institutions in the community to any significant degree. In addition, the general public lacks the training, and often the language skills, necessary to take full advantage of the system. The unique challenge in our region is, therefore, (1) to extend connectivity and the expertise associated with it to community organizations, rural and inner-city schools, senior centers, and similar institutions, while at the same time (2) developing a human, multicultural network of volunteer trainers. The information infrastructure implementation planning process we propose will result in (1) development of a network of trainers; (2) an increasing number of access points in senior centers, community organizations, and schools; and, ultimately, (3) an improvement in the level of job skills, citizen participation in community affairs, and adult literacy."

**Partnerships and Community Support**

> **Planning projects will be evaluated against seven criteria. While each criterion is weighted equally, the following criterion is one of the two qualifying criteria: Problem Definition and Partnerships and Community Support. Planning project applicants must fully meet each qualifying criterion. If an application is deemed inadequate on either of these, it will not be further evaluated.**

Proposals must provide evidence of public and private sector support and involvement. The extent to which applicants have included diverse sectors of the community in project design and development will be considered an integral part of the proposal.

A proposal should present a clear discussion of who the partners will be, what their respective roles in the project will be, what benefits each expects to receive, and what each partner will apply to the project in the form of cash contributions, personnel, or other resources. In addition to identifying and describing project partners, an applicant must provide documentation of the partners' commitment to the project, such as letters from the partners to the applicant describing their roles and contributions. If you have worked with these partners on projects in the past, discuss the nature and results of those projects and the project responsibilities assumed by each collaborator.

## Reducing Disparities in Access to and Use of the NII

In this section, you should identify the existing disparities in access, using specific supporting quantitative and/or demographic data, and describe the barriers to access that cause the disparity. Barriers to access may be geographic, linguistic, cultural, physical, or economic in nature.

Include in this section a profile of the community or communities to be served and the intended beneficiaries of the project. In this profile, cite supporting statistics (e.g., per capita income, percent of households living in poverty, population density, size of the region, etc.), as appropriate. In addition, maps or other geographical representations of the project's impact may be useful in describing the project.

Finally, you should describe the specific steps which you will use to accommodate the particular conditions in the community and to overcome the specific barriers to access or use of the NII that the community faces.

## Applicant Qualifications

Use this section to describe the qualifications of the participating institutions, the key personnel associated with the project, their relationship to the applicant organization, and the applicant's experience in addressing information-related issues. Experience may be demonstrated in a variety of ways, including projects successfully completed and participation in comprehensive planning activities. This does not mean that all applicants must have successfully completed projects similar to, or identical to, the project being proposed; nor does it require that all key personnel must already be employed by one of the participating organizations. The applicant may propose hiring, or contracting with, individuals possessing the relevant expertise. In these instances, however, it is imperative that the proposal describe in detail the qualifications of individuals who would be hired or contracted with during the project award period. If specific individuals have not yet been selected to hold key positions in the project, you should provide brief position descriptions and discussions of expected qualifications for those positions.

In addition, each applicant should present evidence that it is not only a capable organization, but that it is an appropriate and credible organization to undertake the project it proposes.

**Support for End Users**

Expanding upon the problem definition, you should provide a precise definition of the end user population to be served. Demographic or other relevant statistical information on the end user population should be included. Discuss the steps you will take to assess end user needs and demand for the applications you envision, as well as the degree to which you will involve end user groups in the planning process.

**Evaluation and Dissemination**

The evaluation plan that you present should refer to the goals and outcomes described in **Section 1 (Problem Definition),** describe what indicators you will use to determine the success of the planning process, and tell how you will measure them. You should discuss how you will evaluate the planning process and the plan that is developed. Plans for outcome evaluations should also include the capability of documenting and analyzing unexpected outcomes. In presenting your plans, be sure to discuss the evaluation tools (e.g., on-line surveys, focus groups) you intend to employ. You must also identify the people that will be responsible for conducting the evaluation and describe their qualifications if you have not already done so in the section on "Applicant Qualifications."

This section must also include a presentation of your plans for disseminating information about your project and the lessons that you learn during the planning process. Be as specific as possible if you are planning on presenting at conferences, identify the conferences; if you plan to publish articles on the project, identify the journals to which you intend to submit papers.

---

> ## Applicants in Planning Projects should now read the following section, "Instructions for Preparing a Budget Request."

---

## H. INSTRUCTIONS FOR PREPARING A BUDGET REQUEST

The applicant must fully explain each budget item, including both the Federal and non-Federal shares of the total project cost, in the specific and prescribed manner outlined in this section. The budget must be reasonable for the tasks proposed, and the relationship of items in the budget to the project narrative must be clearly drawn.

TIIAP requires that applicants submit three documents to support the budget request:

- Standard Form 424A, *Budget Information—Non-Construction Programs*
- Budget Narrative
- Statement of Matching Funds

Instructions for preparing these documents are provided below. Applicants may also submit an additional budget summary in table (i.e. spreadsheet) form.

Applicants should be aware that grant activities are governed by a variety of federal regulations as described in the footnote below. TIIAP requires detailed budget information so that we can carefully evaluate the cost components of your proposal.[2]

The following instructions for preparing a budget proposal are divided into four sections. The first section describes how the federal government classifies project costs and provides general guidelines and examples of the types of costs that are associated with each category. The second section offers detailed instructions about how to fill out **Standard Form 424A**, the standard federal budget summary form. The third section describes how to prepare the **Budget Narrative** and provides instructions, including examples, about the level of detail required to present and justify different project costs. The discussion of the Budget Narrative is organized according to the federal cost categories that appear in Standard Form 424A. The final section presents guidelines for preparing the **Statement of Matching Funds** and includes an example.

## Overview of Federal Project Cost Categories in Standard Form 424A, *Budget Information*
*—Non-Construction Programs*

The federal government classifies all project costs into "object class categories." These object class categories appear as line items a through j, in Box 6 on the Standard Form 424A. Applicants should break down all project costs into these categories. The object class categories are described below.

### Personnel—Line 6a of the 424A
TIIAP will support salary and fringe benefit expenses for positions directly related to the proposed project. Full-time, salaried positions are eligible costs for federal support only when the position is devoted full-time to the project. This section should not include consultants or staff of contractor organizations. These should be shown under "Contractual" on line 6f.

### Fringe Benefits—Line 6b
This section should include only the fringe benefits, such as health insurance, social security, workers compensation, and retirement benefits, that apply to the personnel claimed in the section on personnel costs. Fringe benefits should be described in detail. Note that if fringe benefits are included in the organization's overall indirect cost rate, then they should not be included in this section, but presented with "Indirect Charges."

### Travel—Line 6c
TIIAP will support travel costs directly related to the project. You must itemize these costs in the budget narrative (see example, page 32). Do not include consultant travel costs in this section, but in the "Contractual" section.

### Equipment—Line 6d
Equipment will typically include computer and telecommunications hardware (e.g., computers, modems, routers, video teleconferencing systems). Software should not be listed in this section (it is listed under "Other"). List items such as floppy disks and magnetic tapes under "Supplies."

### Supplies—Line 6e
Office supplies directly necessary for the project should be listed in this section.

### Contractual—Line 6f
All contractual services, including services provided by individual consultants, should be described in this section.

### Construction—Line 6g
There should be no items listed for construction costs. Construction costs are not eligible in TIIAP.

## Other—Line 6h
Examples of costs appropriately detailed in this section, if not included in indirect costs, include:

- purchase of off-the-shelf software
- charges for telecommunication services such as leased data lines, switched digital services, or Internet access
- charges for information services, such as subscriptions to on-line databases telephone charges
- postage
- photocopying and printing
- office space, if being leased
- leased office equipment and/or furniture
- advertising and/or publicity expenses

## Indirect Charges—Line 6j
"Indirect costs" refer to those costs incurred for common or joint objectives of an organization that cannot be readily identified with a particular or final cost objection. A cost may not be allocated to an award as an indirect cost if any other cost incurred for the same purpose in like circumstances has been assigned to an award as a direct cost. Because of diverse characteristics and accounting practices, it is not possible to specify the types of costs which may be classified as indirect costs in all situations. However, typical examples of indirect costs for many organizations include general administration and general expenses, such as the salaries and expenses of executive officers, personnel administration, maintenance, library expenses, and accounting. Indirect costs are typically charged as a percentage of direct costs. Indirect costs may be included in the TIIAP budget request. The indirect cost rate may not exceed 100% of direct costs and, if the applicant has a current negotiated indirect cost rate with a cognizant federal agency, the rate may exceed the negotiated rate. If you do not have a negotiated rate, the Office of the Inspector General (OIG) is authorized to negotiate indirect cost rates on behalf of the Department of Commerce for those organizations for which the Department of Commerce is cognizant. In these cases, the recipient shall submit to the OIG within 90 days of the award start date, documentation (indirect cost proposal, cost allocation plan, etc.) necessary to establish such rates.

## Instructions for Completing Standard Form 424A, *Budget Information Non-Construction Programs*

### Required for All Applicants

Standard Form 424A is the budget summary form required by the Department of Commerce. The 424A provides reviewers with a quick capsule view of the proposed allocation of project funds.

### Instructions:

### Section A—BUDGET SUMMARY

**Line 1:** Enter the total funds requested from NTIA on line 1, column (e). This number should match the amount entered in Box 15a of the 424.

Enter the amount of non-federal funds, including those from the applicant, state or local governments, or other non-Federal sources, on line 1, column (f).

Enter the sum of columns (e) and (f) in column (g).

Leave blank columns (c) and (d).

**Lines 2-4:** Leave blank.

**Line 5:** Enter the same amounts entered on line 1.

# Section B—Budget Categories

**Column (1):** Enter the NTIA request for each budget category. Note that the total entered in 6k (1) should equal the amount entered in 1 (e) from Section A.

**Column (2):** Enter the non-federal contribution for each budget category. The total entered in 6k (2) should equal the amount entered in 1 (f) from Section A.

**Columns (3) and (4):** Leave blank.

**Column (5):** Enter the sums of columns (1) and (2).

**Line 7:** Leave blank.

## Section C—NON-FEDERAL RESOURCES

**Line 8:** Enter the amount of funds to be contributed by your organization in column (b), funds to be contributed by any state governments in (c), and funds from any other sources in (d). Enter the total in column (e). The total should match the amount entered in Section A, line 1, column f. Enter the same amounts on line 12.

**Lines 9-11:** Leave blank.

## Section D—FORECASTED CASH NEEDS

**Line 13:** Enter the estimated funds that will be required from NTIA for each quarter during the first year of the project.

**Line 14:** Enter the estimated amount of non-Federal contributions that will be made for each quarter of the first year. Note that the Department of Commerce requires that matching funds be expended at about the same rate as federal funds.

## Section E—BUDGET ESTIMATES OF FEDERAL FUNDS NEEDED FOR BALANCE OF PROJECT

**Line 16:** In column (b), enter the estimated total amount of funds that will be required from NTIA for the remainder of the project (i.e., in months 9-24). Enter the same amount in column (b) on line 20.

## Section F—OTHER BUDGET INFORMATION

Leave blank. However, TIIAP requires a Budget Narrative and a Statement of Matching Funds (see below) as attachments to Standard Form 424A.

A sample Standard Form 424A is shown on the following page.

## Instructions for Preparing Budget Narrative

### Required for All Applicants

A detailed Budget Narrative is essential for THAP and its proposal reviewers to analyze the proposed project and the reasonableness of the budget request.

### Instructions:

The Budget Narrative should be organized along the object class categories listed on Standard Form 424A and discussed on page 25 of the Guidelines. Within each category, budget items should be described and justified.

The Budget Narrative should be placed after Standard Form 424A. The pages should be numbered 424A-1, 424A-2, etc.

### Personnel Line 6a of Standard Form 424A

Each staff position for which expenses will be claimed should be listed, by name or by position title. Each listing should contain the position's expected level of effort (e.g., 75%, or 30 hours per week), the duration of the position's involvement (e.g., 18 months), the position's base salary or wage rate (e.g., $35,000 per year, $12 per hour), and a description of the activities to be performed by the person in that position **for the proposed project.** A breakdown of Federal and non-Federal funds for each position should be included. The final tally in each category should include separate totals for both federal and non-federal funds, and a combined total for the entire category. The <u>Statement of Matching Funds</u> (see page 38 for the Guidelines) must have corresponding amounts indicated for each category.

---

*Example:*

**PERSONNEL**

**Project Director:** The Project Director will oversee all aspects of the grant. Responsibilities will include ensuring that budget and timetable targets are met, selecting contractors, putting together an advisory committee, preparing project reports, working with the evaluation consultant to develop the project evaluation, and supervising the project staff. The Project Director will work 25% of the time for 18 months. Based on an annual salary of $60,000, the cost to the project will be $22,500.

Federal Funds: $22,500 Matching Funds: $0 Total: $22,500

**End User Trainer:** The End User Trainer will design and develop curricula, and conduct training classes for end users at each of the 12 project sites. The Trainer will be assigned 100% of the time to the project for the first 12 months and 50% for the remaining 6 months. Based on an annual salary of $24,000, the total project cost will be $30,000.

Federal Funds: $8,000   Matching Funds: $22,000   Total: $30,000

Total Federal Funds:     $30,500
Total Matching Funds:    $22,000

Total Personnel Cost:    $ 52,50

---

### Fringe Benefits—Line 6b

Costs for fringe benefits are typically expressed as a percentage of the base salary or an actual costs. Applicants should list the benefits included in the total fringe calculation.

*Example:*

**FRINGE BENEFITS**

Fringe benefits are calculated as 28.5% of base salary. Benefits include health care, Social Security, workers compensation, short-term disability, and retirement benefits.

```
Project Director          28.5% of $22,500        $6,413

Federal Funds: $0         Matching Funds: $6,413  Total: $6,413


End User Trainer          28.5% of $30,000        $8,550

Federal Funds: $2,280     28.5% of $30,000        Total: $8,550

Federal Funds: $2,280     Matching Funds: $6,270  Total: $8,550

Total Federal Funds:         $ 2,280
Total Matching Funds:        $12,683

Total Fringe Benefits Cost:  $14,963
```

## Travel—Line 6c

Travel expenses must be itemized and calculations shown in detail. Applicants must provide strong justification for any travel expenses proposed for the project. Such justification must show that the proposed travel is necessary to the eventual success of the project. For air travel, the origin, destination, and the estimated air fare should be included. Lodging expenses should include the nightly rate and the number of nights. Meals should be broken out on a per day or per meal basis, as appropriate. Automobile travel should include a standard mileage rate and estimated mileage. The purpose of each travel item must be explained.

*Example:*

**TRAVEL**

**End User Training:** The trainer will make six round trips to each of the twelve sites to conduct training classes for a total of 72 trips. Based on an average of 40 miles round-trip driving at our organization's standard rate of $0.25 per mile, the total cost is $720.

**Meeting with Project Consultants:** The Project Director will fly to city A to meet with project consultants and to tour a similar installation. The estimated round-trip air fare is $900. Ground transportation to and from the hotel will be $50. Two nights lodging will be $180 and two days of meals at the standard per diem will total $76. Total cost: $1,206.

```
Total Federal Funds:       $  963
Total Matching Funds:      $  963

Total Travel Cost:         $1,926
```

## Equipment—Line 6d

All expected equipment purchases should be itemized in this section. If detailed information, such as the manufacturer and model number of configuration details, is available, it should be included. However, as shown in the example below, exhaustive detail is not required. Each equipment item (or set of items) should be justified. Applicants may also wish to include a summary itemized list of equipment to be purchased.

*Example:*

**EQUIPMENT**

**Personal Computers:** One personal computer will be installed at each of 12 sites for public access to the network. Each computer will be equipped with a high-speed modem and a CD-ROM drive and will cost $2,000.

```
Federal Funds: $0          Matching Funds: $24,000      Total: $24,000
```

**Network Server:** A GreatServer 2,000 network server will be located at the project headquarters. The server will be the repository of the local information files and will manage the electronic mail communication among the sites. The server will be configured with a 1 GB hard drive, 32 MB of RAM, and have a magnetic tape drive for backup purposes. Cost: $14,498.

```
Federal Funds: $14,498     Matching Funds: $0           Total: $14,498
```

**Network Router:** A network router will be located at the headquarters of the site. The router will manage communications with the external network. The cost of the router is estimated at $3,500.

```
Federal Funds: $3,500      Matching Funds: $0           Total: $3,500
```

| Item | Quantity | Unit Price | Total |
|------|----------|-----------|-------|
| personal computers | 12 | $2,000 | $24,000 |
| network server | 1 | $14,498 | $14,498 |
| network router | 1 | $3,500 | $3,500 |
| Total Federal Funds: | | $17,998 | |
| Total Matching Funds: | | $24,000 | |
| Total Equipment Cost: | | $41,998 | |

**Supplies—Line 6e**

To the extent practicable, costs for supplies should be itemized.

*Example:*

**SUPPLIES**

Office supplies such as paper, pens and pencils, diskettes, laser printer cartridges, staplers, file folders, etc. are estimated at $750.

| | |
|---|---|
| Total Federal Funds: | $375 |
| Total Matching Funds: | $375 |
| Total Supplies Cost: | $750 |

**Contractual—Line 6f**

Each service should be described in detail. The costs should be explained and justified. Any proposed single source contract under the award must be stipulated and a complete sole source justification must be provided.

> *Example:*
>
> **CONTRACTUAL**
>
> **Network Installation and Maintenance:** A vendor will be competitively selected to install and provide 12 months of ongoing maintenance for the project's network. Installation will include the assembly and configuration of the public access computers, the server, the router, connection to network circuits, and overall system testing. Based on inquiries to local vendors, it is estimated that 100 hours, at $75 per hour will be required for the installation and a 24-hour response maintenance contract is estimated at $200 per month. Total cost: $9,900.
>
> ```
> Federal Funds: $9,900      Matching Funds: $0      Total: $9,900
> ```
>
> **Evaluation Consultant:** An expert in evaluating the impact of networks such as the one proposed in this project will be chosen to develop an evaluation plan, design the evaluation survey instruments, analyze evaluation data, and prepare a report. It is estimated that the consultant will work for 25 days at a rate of $800 per day. Total cost: $20,000.
>
> ```
> Federal Funds: $0          Matching Funds: $20,000   Total: $20,000
>
> Total Federal Funds:       $9,900
> Total Matching Funds:      $20,000
>
> Total Contractual Cost:    $29,900
> ```

**Other—Line 6h**

All costs must be itemized. No miscellaneous or contingency costs are acceptable. Each item must be justified and its relationship to the project's completion explained. (See Example.)

> *Example:*
>
> **Other**
>
> **Telephone service for the volunteer help desk.** Twelve months @ $25 per month, for a total of $300.
>
> **Software for the network server: The network server will require a single license of each of the following software packages in order to run the community network:**
>
> ```
>     CoolMail mail handler: $995
>     Manage-My-Net network management software: $495
> ```
>
> **Leased T-1 circuit:** This circuit will be used to connect the network to the Internet service provider, twelve months @ $460 per month: $5,520.
>
> **Photocopier:** The project will be leasing a photocopier for 18 months at a rate of $50 per month for a total of $900.
>
> ```
> Total Federal Funds:       $4,105
> Total Matching Funds:      $4,105
>
> Total Other Costs:         $8,210
> ```

**Indirect Charges—Line 6j**

In this section of the Budget Narrative, the applicant should explain how the indirect rate is applied to the direct costs. In the simplest case, the indirect rate is a percentage that is applied to all direct costs. However, some organizations apply indirect costs only to certain categories of direct costs, in which case an explanation of how the total amount is derived is helpful. If the applicant has a negotiated indirect cost rate, the agreement must be attached to the Budget Narrative. If the applicant does not have a negotiated rate, a separate sheet (or sheets) detailing the calculation of the indirect rate must be attached to the Budget Narrative. If an indirect cost rate has not been established by the applicant with its Cognizant Federal Agency, the applicant will be required to establish one in order to claim indirect costs under an award.

It is important to note that, in some instances, contracted services expenditures include indirect charges as part of the cost. Indirect costs for contracted services should be included under the "Contractual" section in the Budget and Budget Narrative, not under the "Indirect Charges" section. The "Indirect Charges" section should only include indirect costs to be charged by the applicant. (See example below.)

---

*Example:*

**INDIRECT CHARGES**

<organization name> applies an indirect cost rate of 22.5% to all direct cost categories except equipment. No indirect charges are applied to equipment costs. A copy of <organization name> current negotiated indirect cost rate with the U.S. Department of Health and Human Services is attached.

```
Total Direct Charges (except equipment):        $108,249
Total Indirect Costs @ 22.5%:                   $24,356

Federal Funds:              $12,126
Matching Funds:             $12,230

Total Indirect Charges:     $24,356
```

---

**Instructions for Preparing Statement of Matching Funds**

**Required for All Applicants**

A project will not be considered eligible for funding unless the applicant documents the capacity to supply matching funds. Applications that do not meet this requirement will be rejected.

The Statement of Matching Funds is essential for reviewers and TIIAP staff to understand which project costs identified in Standard Forms 424 and 424A and in the Budget Narrative will be supported by which organizations. The Statement of Matching Funds also identifies which matching funds are cash and which are in-kind contributions.

---

**The funds provided as the non-Federal share are subject to the same administrative requirements, cost principles, and audit requirements as the Federal share.**

---

**Instructions:**

Matching funds are divided into two categories: (1) cash contributions and (2) in-kind contributions. The funds the applicant has identified as the non-federal matching share on the Standard Forms 424 and 424A should be fully described and broken down into "cash" and "in-kind" contributions, as shown on page 38 in the sample Statement of Matching Funds.

Cash contributions are further broken down into (1) direct monetary contributions from any non-Federal source and (2) personnel services provided by the applicant. Salaries for personnel working on the project as paid by the applicant from non-Federal funds are considered cash contributions.

In-kind contributions are generally in the form of donated property, equipment, space, personnel services, or contracted services from third party sources. These contributions may be computers, evaluation or financial management services, or other services or property provided by institutions other than the grantee.

Note that all funds listed in the Statement of Matching Funds must correspond **exactly** to cost items discussed in the Budget Narrative. Matching funds must be **itemized** with the same level of detail as the Federal costs. With respect to in-kind donations, it is essential to remember that an item which is not eligible for Federal support **cannot** be included as a match.

The applicant should indicate whether the funds will be available at the time of award or if they are to be collected at a later date. If the funds are to be raised through mechanisms such as service or registration fees or other anticipated program income, this should be indicated. The applicant should provide appropriate, specific documentation on letterhead from sources of matching funds, certifying that they will provide the funds indicated in the Statement of Matching Funds. These letters should be inserted into the proposal directly after the Statement of Matching Funds.

As discussed in the Notice, NTIA will provide 50% of the total project unless special circumstances warrant a grant of up to 75%.

---

**Applicants requesting more than the standard NTIA share of 50% should use the Statement of Matching Funds to explain fully the reasons for the request and, if possible, provide appropriate supporting documentation.**

---

*Example:*

**Statement of Matching Funds**

The matching funds will consist of <organization name>'s own funds and in-kind contributions of consulting services from the <contributor 1 name>, and computer equipment from the <contributor 1 name>. A summary of the matching funds and the NTIA request is provided below.

**Cash Contributions from <organization name>**

- $28,913 in salary and fringe for the end user trainer
- $963 for travel
- $375 for supplies
- $4,105 for other costs
- $12,230 in indirect charges

- Total cash Contribution: $46,586

**In-Kind Contribution from <contributor 1 name>**

<contributor 1 name> will provide the services of an evaluation consultant for 25 days. These services are valued at $800 per day for a total contribution of $20,000.

**In-Kind Contribution from <contributor 2 name>**

<contributor 2 name> will donate 12 personal computers, valued at $2,000, for a total contribution of $24,000.

**NTIA Request**

<organization name> requests that NTIA provide grant funds to cover the following costs:

- $38,500 in salary and fringe for the project coordinator
- $963 for travel
- $375 for supplies
- $17,998 for equipment
- $9,900 for contractual costs
- $4,105 for other costs
- $12,126 in indirect costs

- total NTIA request: $84,017

**J. Instructions for Completing Standard Form CD-511,** *Certifications Regarding Debarment, Suspension, and Other Responsibility Matters; Drug-Free Workplace Requirements and Lobbying*

**Required for All Applicants**

The Department of Commerce requires that all applicants certify that they are complying with certain conditions put on the award of federal assistance.

**Instructions:**

An original signature is required on the back of form CD-511, Certifications. Include the date signed. This form should be signed by the same person who signs the form 424.

**K. Instructions for Completing Standard Form LLL,** *Disclosure of Lobbying Activities*

**Required for all applicants who are engaged in lobbying the federal government on behalf of their application**

This form is used to disclose any lobbying activities in which the applicant is engaged on behalf of the application.

**Instructions:**

The filing of the form is required for each payment or an agreement to make a payment to any lobbying entity for influencing or attempting to influence an officer or employee of any agency, a member of Congress, an officer or employee of Congress, or an employee of a member of Congress in connection with the application.

The instructions for completing Standard Form LLL are provided on the back of the form.

**L. Instructions for Completing Standard Form CD-346,** *Application for Federal Assistance*

**Required for all non-governmental applicants except for accredited colleges and universities**

Representatives of state and local government entities, including school districts and public libraries, and of accredited colleges and universities do not need to submit CD-346 forms.

Under Department of Commerce regulations, TIIAP must request that key personnel in the project fill out the Form CD-346, the purpose of which is to determine the character and integrity of principle officers and employees in the applicant's organization.

**Instructions:**

An original signature and date are required at the bottom of the page. Each of the following project members should fill out and sign the CD-346:

- the executive director of the organization (or president, CEO, or other similar title)
- the chief financial officer of the organization
- the project director, project manager, or principle investigator for the TIIAP proposal

**M. Additional Materials**

Applicants may attach additional materials that are relevant to their applications. However, you are strongly encouraged to use restraint in submitting additional materials with your application; keep in mind that it cannot be more than 40 pages in length, excluding the Standard Federal forms and all budget information.

## APPENDIX I—LIST OF STATE SINGLE POINTS OF CONTACT

## APPENDIX I—APPLICATION FORMS

This section contains the following application forms needed to complete a TIIAP application:

- Standard Form 424, *Application for Federal Assistance*
- Standard Form 424A, *Budget Information—Non-Construction Programs*
- Standard Form 424B, *Assurances*
- Standard Form CD-511, *Certifications Regarding Debarment, Suspension, and Other Responsibility Matters; Drug-Free Workplace Requirements and Lobbying*
- Standard Form LLL, *Disclosure of Lobbying Activities*
- Standard Form CD-346, *Applicant for Funding Assistance*

Instructions for completing these forms are provided in the section on "Completing the TIIAP Application," on pages 2-40 of the Guidelines.

## Please use photocopies of these application forms for your application and save the original copies for use in case TIIAP requests revisions during its review.

## Application Checklist

Please use the following checklist to assist you in reviewing your 1996 TIIAP application before submitting it. The checklist will help ensure the completeness of your application and its compliance with TIIAP requirements. DO NOT RETURN THIS CHECKLIST.

- Have you allowed sufficient time for the complete proposal package to be **received by TIIAP** no later than close of business (5:00 p.m., Eastern Standard Time), Thursday, April 4, 1996?
- Have you included **one (1) original and five copies** of the application? Have you **stapled the original?** Have you **stapled one (1) of the copies and binder clipped each of the four (4) other looseleaf copies?**
- Do the original copies of each required form have **easily identifiable original signatures?**
- Have you included an **Executive Summary** of your project? Does the first sentence of the Summary contain the **Category (Demonstration, Access,** or **Planning)** and the **primary application area (and, if applicable, the secondary application area)?**
- Is the **Project Narrative** within the required page limit, [6 (six) pages for Demonstration projects, 5 (five) pages for Access projects, 5 (five) pages for Planning projects?
- Are the figures presented in the **Budget Narrative,** the required **Standard Form 424A,** and the required **Standard Form 424, Box 15(a)-(g)** in agreement? Did you check the math?
- Have the pages of the proposal been **properly numbered?** Have you taken care **to not exceed the 40 page limit?**
- Have you **completed** and **signed** the required Standard Forms (SF-424, SF-424A, SF-424B, CD-511, and, if applicable, SF-LLL and CD-346)?
- Have you included the **Legal Name of the Organization** in Standard Form 424, Box 5?
- Have you included the **complete Street Address (not a Post Office Box)** in Standard Form 424, Box 5?

- Have you provided a **telephone number** and, if available, a **fax number** and **e-mail address?**
- Have you followed the prescribed format for **project start date** and **project end date** (Box 13) in Standard Form 424?
- Have you included the **Category, Primary Application Area,** and **Project Title** in Standard Form 424, Box 11? Are the category and primary application area worded exactly as they appear in these *Guidelines?*
- Have you included a **single Congressional District** in Standard Form 424, Box 14a?

---

## Footnotes

<1> Under the heading **Project Funding Priorities,** the <u>Notice of Solicitation of Grant Applications</u> defines four broad application groups, and places all three of the following areas—Preschool and K-12 Education, Higher Education, and Library and Lifelong Learning Services—under the group Lifelong Learning. Similarly, the *Notice* places Human Services and Public under the Public Services group. However, for the purposes of these *Guidelines,* and to facilitate a more efficient review of your proposal, **you must select a specific application area from the list of seven application areas.** Therefore, if your proposal best fits into the application area of Pre-School and K-12 Education, you must *select* "Pre-School and K-12 Education" as the appropriate application area, rather than simply indicating Lifelong Learning

<2> Upon receipt of a grant, all grantees are subject to federal regulations and governing aspects of the grantor/grantee relationship. The specific regulations governing the grant will depend on the nature of the entity receiving the grant, *i.e.,* state or local government, nonprofit institution, or institutions of higher education. These regulations include, but are not necessarily limited to, Department of Commerce Financial Assistance Standard Terms and Conditions and any Special Award Conditions; 15 CFR Part 24, Uniform Administrative Requirements for Grants and Cooperative Agreements to State and Local Governments; 15 CFR Part 29a, Audit Requirements for State and Local Governments; 15 CFR Part 29b, Audit Requirements for Institutions of Higher Education and Other Nonprofit Organizations; 48 CFR Part 31, Contract Cost Principles and Procedures; and Office of Management and Budget (OMB) Circular A-21 Cost Principles for Educational Institutions; OMB Circular A-87, Cost Principles for State and Local Governments; OMB Circular A-110, Grants and Agreements with Institutions of Higher Education, Hospitals, and Other Nonprofit Organizations; and 45 CFR Part 74, Appendix E. In the event that an applicant is offered a grant, the Department of Commerce will inform the entity which of the above regulations are applicable.

Source: U.S. Department of Commerce
National Telecommunications and Information Administration
Office of Telecommunications and Information Applications
Revised: 02/29/96

# Analyzing Real Grant Proposals

## Grant #4—Questions

1. What are the three application categories?

   _____

   _____

   _____

2. What are the seven application areas?

   _____

   _____

   _____

   _____

   _____

   _____

   _____

3. What is Standard Form 424?

   _____

   _____

   _____

4. What does NTIA stand for?

   _____

5. What is the TIIAP?

   _____

6. Why is the authorized representative directed to sign Form 424 in blue ink?

_____

7. What is the primary goal of Demonstration projects?

_____

_____

_____

8. What is the primary goal of Access projects?

_____

_____

_____

9. What is the primary goal of Planning projects?

_____

_____

_____

10. What is the Budget Narrative and where should it be placed in the application?

_____

_____

_____

11. Did you have any problems with this set of guidelines?

_____

_____

_____

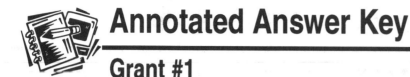

# Annotated Answer Key

## Grant #1

1. Telephone number: (213) 662-5237

2. FAX number: No FAX number is given.

3. Mailing address:     Dianne Glinos, Grants Manager
                            Los Angeles Educational Partnership
                            315 W. Ninth Street, Suite 1110
                            Los Angeles, CA 90015

4. Number of Pages:
        Minimum Number Required: 4
        Maximum Number Allowed: 4 or 5

(This is confusing. In the "Application Requirement" it says no more than four pages will be accepted, but at the bottom of page C we are told an additional page may be submitted if the application includes more than four teachers.)

Attachments Allowed: No. Just the additional page mentioned above.

5. Layout of Pages:

Applications must be typed or computer printed in black ink only.

No other formatting criteria are given but, presumably, everything must fit into the spaces on the form.

6. Title:

There is a space for the title.

7. Abstract:

A summary is asked for twice, once in "I. Project Summary and Objectives" and again on page D. The summary on page D sounds more like an abstract because of plans to print it in the Grant Catalogue.

8. Table of Contents:

No table of contents because of page limitations.

9. Introduction:

There is no separate place for an introduction, so it will simply be the beginning of the narrative.

10. Goal/Vision/Mission:

Not required and no place for it.

11. Statement of Needs:

This application jumps directly to objectives.

12. Objectives:

Student outcome objectives are asked for in the first section.

13. Activities:

Student activities are asked for in the second section.

14. Management:

    Management of the project is built into the second section.

15. Personnel:

    Except for the information to be written on page C, all personnel information is included in the second section.

16. Timelines:

    The timeline (brief, estimated) goes in the second section too.

17. Resources:

    Resources are in "III. Budget."

18. Evaluation:

    There is no place for a formal evaluation plan.

19. Dissemination:

    There is no dissemination requirement. The project will be shared through a catalogue which will describe all of the projects and be distributed locally and nationally.

20. Budget:

    The budget is covered in the third section.

21. Attachment:

    No attachments are allowed. See page limitations.

---

## Page 121

1. The grant application could be submitted by e-Mail but not by FAX.

2. Los Angeles Educational Partnership.

3. World Wide Web address: http:/www.lalc.k12.ca.us/

4. e-mail address: grants lalc.k12.ca.us.

5. Applications were due by 5:00 P.M. on April 25, 1996.

6. Grant applications were to be submitted by teams of at least two teachers.

7. Up to $500 could be awarded for each accepted grant.

8. Major funding was provided by Toyota USA Foundation for Toyota Innovation Grants in Math and Science.

9. SMART is an acronym for Science and Math Advancement Resources for Teachers.

10. Applicants could not pay for any of the project themselves.

# Annotated Answer Key

## Grant #2

---

### Page 122

1. Telephone number: (202) 457-0588

2. FAX number: (202) 296-1098 (No proposals will be accepted by FAX)

3. Mailing address:   Partnership for Education and Economic Opportunity
   The Hitachi Foundation
   1509 22nd Street N.W.
   Washington, D.C. 20037-1073

---

### Page 124

4. Number of Pages:
   Minimum Number Required: 4
   Maximum Number Allowed: 6 plus specified attachments
   Attachments Allowed: Required
   - timeline for proposed activities
   - overall project budget
   - primary project personnel/qualifications
   - letters of commitment
   - copy of 501 (c)(3) tax exempt notification letter
   - cover sheet

5. Layout of Pages:
   4-6 pages, single or double-spaced
   no other specifications

---

### Page 125

6. Title:
   There is no mention of a project title and no space for it on the cover sheet.

7. Abstract:
   An abstract is not required.

8. Table of Contents:
   A table of contents is not required.

9. Introduction:
   There is no separate place for an introduction, so it will simply be the beginning of the narrative.

10. Goal/Vision/Mission:
    The last item in the 4–6 page description of the project asks for a statement of organizational mission.

11. Statement of Needs:
    The fourth item in the 4–6 page description of the project asks for a description of the target population and its size, and the specific challenges and issues it faces.

12. Objectives:

    The third item in the 4–6 page description includes project objectives.

13. Activities:

    The third item in the 4–6 page description includes specific activities.

14. Management:

    Management of the project is implied in the requirements for the 4-6 page description.

15. Personnel:

    See attachments.

16. Timelines:

    See attachments.

17. Resources:

    No specific mention.

18. Evaluation:

    Proposed evaluation criteria for the project are to be included in the 4-6 page description.

19. Dissemination:

    The Hitachi Foundation disseminates program results.

20. Budget:

    The budget appears as an attachment.

21. Attachments:

    Required attachments are listed in Formatting Issues above.

## Page 132

1. $100,000 to $300,000 for individual projects.

2. The Foundation expects to make grants to 4-6 organizations.

3. The organizations receiving funding will be "diverse in location, character of collaboration, person, stages of program development, and methods in achieving program goals."

4. The Hitachi foundation fund does not fund individual schools. Schools are funded as part of community partnerships.

5. The Hitachi Foundation is "a nonprofit, philanthropic organization with a mission to promote social responsibility through effective participation in a global society."

6. The second deadline is for full proposals from top candidates.

7. The contact person for grant information is Jeanette Rogers, Program Assistant.

# Annotated Answer Key

## Grant #3

1. Telephone number: (202) 606-8373 Staff

2. FAX number: (202) 606-8394

3. Mailing address:   Division of Research and Education, Room 302
                      National Endowment for the Humanities
                      1100 Pennsylvania Avenue N.W.
                      Washington, D.C. 20506

4. Number of Pages

   Minimum Number Required: cover sheet, table of contents, one page summary, detailed narrative, project, budget, and appendices.

   Maximum Number Allowed: narrative should not exceed 20 pages.

   Attachments Allowed: Appendices as necessary

5. Layout of Pages:

   type (double-spaced) on white 8 ½" x 11" paper

   create margins and use a type face and size that allows reviewers to read applications easily

   label appendices and number them consecutively

6. Title:

   A descriptive title is to be entered on the cover sheet.

7. Abstract:

   One page summary of the narrative; may be single-spaced.

8. Table of Contents:

   List all sections including appendices.

9. Introduction:

   There is no separate place for an introduction, so it will simply be the beginning of the narrative.

10. Goal/Vision/Mission:

    The first section of the narrative, the "Rationale," asks for an explanation of how the objectives will improve the quality of humanities education.

11. Statement of Needs:

    It looks as if this is supposed to be part of the rationale and institutional context. It is not as clear-cut in this regard as one might like it to be.

12. Objectives:

    The statement of objectives is also just assumed as part of the narrative.

13. Activities:

    The activities are contained in the third section of the narrative.

14. Management:

    Management of the project is included in section four of the narrative, "Project Staff and Participants."

15. Personnel:

    "Project Staff and Participants."

16. Timelines:

    Assumably part of the narrative.

17. Resources:

    "Institutional Context."

18. Evaluation:

    This is found in the fifth section of the narrative, "Evaluation."

19. Dissemination:

    This is found in the sixth section of the narrative, "Follow-up and Dissemination."

20. Budget:

    The budget is a separate section. A separate budget narrative is suggested for large items, and an extensive sample budget is included.

21. Attachments:

    "Use appendices to provide supplementary but essential materials… "

---

## Page 159

1. This is a federal grant.

2. The missing parts are the standard cover sheet and the NEH Budget Form.

3. The three areas for applications are (1) development of new educational materials, (2) field testing and preparing classroom application of new and existing materials, and (3) ways to enable teachers to integrate new materials and approaches into their teaching.

4. The criteria for evaluation are: intellectual quality, worth, and feasibility.

5. Grantees receiving $25,000 or more in federal award during their fiscal year must have an audit performed.

6. No applications are accepted by either e-mail or FAX.

7. The application package must contain twelve copies of the application itself.

1.  Telephone number: (202) 482-2048

2.  FAX number: (202) 501-5136 / e-mail: tiiap ntia.doc.gov

3.  Mailing address:  U.S. Department of Commerce
    National Telecommunications and Information Administration
    Office of Telecommunications and Information Applications
    TIIAP, Room 4090
    14th Street and Constitution Avenue, N.W.
    Washington, D.C. 20230

4.  Number of Pages:

    Minimum Number Required: There are a variety of different required sections, but they could vary in length. There is no stated minimum number of pages.

    Maximum Number Allowed: The page limit is 40 pages including all text, tables, illustrations, maps, letters, references, resumes, and supporting documents, excluding the Standard Forms and all budget information.

    Attachments Allowed: Appendices as necessary, as long as the 40-page limit is not exceeded.

5.  Layout Pages:

    typed, single-spaced on 8 ½" x 11" (22 cm x 28 cm) paper

    using a font of no less than 12 points

    with margins of no less than 1" (2.5 cm)

    pages numbered consecutively starting with the first page of the Project Narrative; the Budget Narrative and Statement of Matching Funds are to be numbered 424A-1, 424A-2, etc.

6.  Title:

    A descriptive title is to be entered on the third line of Box 11 of Standard Form 424 following the category of the application (line one) and the primary application area (line 2).

7.  Abstract:

    Every proposal needs to begin with an Executive Summary which does not exceed 125 words. The first sentence of this summary is prescribed in the instructions.

8.  Table of Contents:

    A table of contents may be inserted after Form 424 and before the Project Narrative.

9.  Introduction:

    There is no separate place for an introduction, so it will simply be the beginning of the narrative.

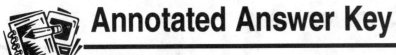

10. Goal/Vision/Mission:

    Goals can be included in the Executive Summary. There is no separate place for a goal statement.

11. Statement of Needs:

    It is called the Problem Definition in this application. "The problem definition must be specific and convincing… (and) thoroughly documented, using comparative data such as statistics."

12. Objectives:

    The statement of objectives seems to be included in the Program Definition: "… and describe the outcomes you expect from your project…"

13. Activities:

    Described in Technical Approach.

14. Management:

    Included in Applicant Qualifications.

15. Personnel:

    Included in Applicant Qualifications.

16. Time Lines:

    Included in Technical Approach. "This section must also include a discussion of the project implementation schedule."

17. Resources:

    Included in Technical Approach.

18. Evaluation:

    This is found in Evaluation and Dissemination, as well as in Ability to Serve as a Model.

19. Dissemination:

    This is found in Evaluation and Dissemination, as well as in Ability to Serve as a Model.

20. Budget:

    The Budget Instructions are a separate section. A Standard Budget Form and a Budget Narrative must be included, as well as a statement of matching funds.

21. Attachments:

    Appendices as necessary, as long as the 40-page limit is not exceeded.

---

## Pages 200 and 201

1. The three application categories are:

   - Demonstration
   - Access
   - Planning

---

2. The seven application areas are:
   - Community-wide Networking
   - Health
   - Pre-School and K-12 Education
   - Higher Education
   - Library and Lifelong Learning Services
   - Human Services
   - Public Safety

3. Standard Form 424 is the face sheet (cover sheet) required on all applications for federal assistance.

4. NTIA stands for National Telecommunications and Information Administration.

5. TIIAP stands for Telecommunications and Information Infrastructure Assistance Program.

6. The authorized representative is directed to sign Form 424 in blue ink so that the original signature can be distinguished from the copies. (Directions for Form 424, Box 18.)

7. The primary goal of Demonstration projects is to demonstrate new, high-impact, useful applications of information infrastructure which hold significant potential for replication in other communities.

8. The primary goal of Access projects is to provide underserved communities, populations, or geographic areas with greater access to the benefits of the National Information Infrastructure (NII).

9. The primary goal of Planning projects is to enable organizations, or groups of organizations, to develop strategies of the enhanced application of information infrastructure.

10. The Budget Narrative is an explanation and justification of the budget. It should be organized along the object class categories listed on Standard Form 424A (Budget Information). Within each category, budget items should be described and justified.

    The Budget Narrative should be placed after Standard Form 424A. The pages should be numbered 424A-1, 424A-2, etc.

11. Some of the problems you might have encountered in using this guideline are:
    - the lack of forms
    - boxed "warnings" that lead to no place in particular
    - specific instructions that seem contradictory

This is one of those grants for which you might want to call the funder.

# Grants For Schools—Part Four

## Table of Contents

# Your Own Grant Writing Workshop

## How to Set It Up

### Back to Committee

Now that you know everything there is to know about other people's grants, it is time to try writing your own grant proposal from start to finish. The most enjoyable way to do this is to stage a Grant Writing Workshop with the knowledge people on the Grant Committee. Send out invitations for a special meeting (page 213).

### Supply Grant Application Guidelines and Forms

If there is an appropriate local grant being offered in your area, get guidelines and application forms from the funding organization (one set for each workshop participant). If not, use the generic guidelines and application form that follow (pages 214–220).

### Create and Supply Needs Scenarios

Get out those survey tabulations from the beginning of this project and look at the identified areas of needs. Create scenarios from them, or make up some. Print out each scenario on a separate piece of paper and pass them out at the first meeting of your Grant Writing Workshop. You can seal each one in an envelope if you want and let people draw them out of a hat.

### Review the Guidelines

Start your workshop by reviewing the Grant Application Guidelines as a group. Discuss the requirements and clarify the concepts. Review the parts of a grant proposal.

### Discuss Ways of Writing

Some people like to write their first drafts in pencil on a yellow pad. Other people like to compose on a computer so they can cut and paste and move things around as they go. Some people will want to work at home all by themselves. Others like the stimulation of a group. Whatever the members of your group like to do, make plans to accommodate everybody. Maybe you can arrange to use your school's computer lab a couple of evenings a week.

### Grant Reading Coming Up

When everyone's needs have been satisfied, schedule a meeting to compare notes and prepare for the Grant Reading Workshop (starting on page 221).

## Committee Invitation

Photocopy this invitation on school letterhead. Use it to invite Grant Committee members to a workshop on writing grants.

------------------------------------------------------------------

Dear

We have reached a new stage in our pursuit of grant money. We are ready to have our own Grant Writing Workshop.

Please plan to attend our meeting to pick up and discuss the materials you will need for this activity.

It should be fun and it will give us all a chance to put what we have learned into action.

Sincerely,

_____

— note —

Meeting place: _____

_____

_____

Meeting time: _____

Comments:

### Needs Scenario

Insert real or fictional data into templates such as these to create a group of needs scenarios.

- - - - - - - - - - - - - - - - - - - - - - - - - - - - - - - - - - - - - - - -

The students of _____ School located in, _____ have

tested in the _____ percentile in_____, as measured by

the _____ test, for the last two years.  Since they show average to above-

average IQs on the _____ test, there is a large discrepancy between intelligence

and performance.  (See Addenda I and II.)

- - - - - - - - - - - - - - - - - - - - - - - - - - - - - - - - - - - - - - - -

Entering kindergarten students of _____ School located in _____,

_____ , show a lack of both academic and social readiness as measured by the

_____ test.  (See Addenda I.) _____ School is in an

economically depressed area with few preschool programs.  Of _____ entering students,

_____ % have qualified for the free lunch program.  There is no breakfast program now in effect at

_____ School.

- - - - - - - - - - - - - - - - - - - - - - - - - - - - - - - - - - - - - - - -

Of _____ graduating seniors at _____ High School,

an academically-focused school in an affluent area, only _____ % of the _____

applying for college admittance were accepted by the college that was their first choice.  The SAT

scores of these same students, ranged from _____ to _____

in math and from _____ to _____ in language arts.

# Your Own Writing Workshop

## The Grant Application Guidelines

Use this generic set of guidelines for the grant application that follows.

---

# Funding Foundation
# Grant Guidelines

### Application Guidelines

1. Complete and attach the cover sheet. Make sure it is signed by the principal or the grant manager.

2. Use only the pages provided and confine your narrative to the spaces provided in each section.

3. Formatting: Do not reduce written materials.
   Use a 12 pt. font with no less than six lines to an inch (2.5 cm).

### Program Description

Please describe your program in the spaces provided on pages 218-220. Include the following information:

1. A brief vision statement

2. Your objectives for this project

3. The activities you plan to use including a time line

4. An evaluation plan

5. An itemized budget

---

# Your Own Grant Writing Workshop

## The Grant Application Guidelines *(cont.)*

Use this generic set of guidelines for the grant application that follows.

# Funding Foundation
# Grant Guidelines *(cont.)*

### Judging Criteria

Your application will be judged against these criteria:

1. Students will be engaged in active learning.

2. The objectives are reasonable and clearly defined.

3. Student activities are described clearly.

4. The evaluation plan is reasonable in scope.

5. The budget reflects the planned activities.

6. The program has the potential for increasing support for public education.

*Note: Funding for this grant is not to exceed $7,500.*

# Your Own Grant Writing Workshop

## The Grant Application Form

Try your hand at this generic grant application.

# Funding Foundation
### *Grant Application—Cover Sheet*

_____
Name of School

_____
Mailing Address

_____
City/Zip Code

_____
School Telephone Number

_____
Name of Program Leader

_____
Program Leader's Telephone Number

_____
Name of Principal

_____
Signature

_____
CDS Number

_____
School District

_____
County

_____
District Mailing Address

_____
City/Zip Code

_____
District Telephone Number

_____
Name of Superintendent

_____
Signature

**Target Population**    Number of Students _____    Number of Teachers _____

Number of Parents _____    Number of Grade Levels _____

**Program Cost:** _____    **Amount Requested:** _____

# Funding Foundation

### *Grant Application—Program Description*

**Title of Program:** _____

**Grant Amount Requested:** _____

**Vision Statement:** _____

_____

_____

_____

_____

_____

*Objectives (Including Population Targeted):*

_____

_____

_____

_____

_____

_____

_____

_____

_____

_____

# Funding Foundation

### *Grant Application—Program Description* *(cont.)*

**Activities** *(Including Time Line):* _____

_____

_____

_____

_____

_____

_____

_____

**Evaluation Plan:** _____

_____

_____

_____

_____

_____

_____

_____

_____

_____

# Funding Foundation

### *Grant Application—Program Description* *(cont.)*

**Itemized Budget:**

Description

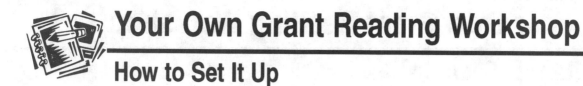

# Your Own Grant Reading Workshop

## How to Set It Up

### Schedule the Workshop

After the members of your Grant Committee have taken their Needs Scenarios, their Grant Writing Guidelines, and their Grant Application Forms away with them, they will need some time to actually write their grants. Do not give them too much time, however, or the project will be lost in the crush of their busy lives and they will wind up putting it off forever.

Set your meeting for the Grant Reading Workshop for no more than two weeks in the future and send reminder notes (page 222).

### Cooperative Learning Time

While grant writing tends to be a solitary business, grant reading is not. This is a group activity. Since you will have reminded everyone not to put his or her own name on the grants and since they will all be in 12 point type, you will be able to preserve the anonymity of all your workshop participants. This is important. Having one's first attempt at writing a grant read publicly by several people can be overwhelming. By the time all the reading is done, some of the self-consciousness will have diminished. However, go over the rules of cooperative learning just as you would in a classroom, especially the one about making only positive statements!

### At Least Two Readers

Grant reading and scoring is done very much the same way as the holistic scoring of any writing sample. All of the readers sit down together and review and discuss the scoring criteria. You will need to make some basic decisions. In real grant reading and scoring, as we have learned, applications are screened for format when they are received. How strict are you going to be? If one of your grant writers used a 10 point font, are you going to throw out the application without reading it? If one of your grant writers neglected to include a budget, will you throw out that application? It is up to you, but once you reach consensus on these decisions, try to stick to them.

Each proposal is read by two different people, the *A reader* and the *B reader*. Code the proposals with numbers and have people record their scores on the A sheet or the B sheet. When all of the proposals have been read by two people, compare the scoring sheets. If the two scores for a proposal are the same, that is the score. If they are different, someone else (the *C reader*) reads the proposal and decides. (See pages 223-226)

### Celebrate Your Efforts

Serve coffee and cookies and let people claim their proposals publicly, if they so choose!

**Reminder Note**

Photocopy this invitation on school letterhead. Use it to invite Grant Committee members to a workshop on reading grants.

------------------------------------------------------------------------------------

Dear Grant Writer,

Bring your completed grant to the Grant Reading Workshop and learn to be a grant reader as well as a grant writer.

Do not put your name on your grant proposal!

Sincerely,

_____

note

Meeting place: _____

_____

_____

Meeting time: _____

Comments:

# Your Own Grant Writing Workshop

## The Grant Scoring Sheet

Use this form to evaluate individual applications.

## Funding Foundation

### Grant Application Score Sheet

Please use one sheet for each application. Use the following criteria to arrive at a score. A maximum of 25 points is possible.

| Criteria | Low 1 | 3 | High 5 |
|---|---|---|---|
| 1. Students will be engaged in active learning. | | | |
| 2. The objectives are reasonable and clearly defined. | | | |
| 3. Student activities are described clearly. | | | |
| 4. The evaluation plan is reasonable in scope. | | | |
| 5. The budget reflects the planned activities. | | | |
| 6. The program has the potential for increasing support for public education. | | | |

**Do you recommend this proposal for funding?** _____

**Comments:**

# Your Own Grant Reading Workshop

## Recording Sheets

Reader A, keep a record of the scores you decide to give to each grant proposal you read.

| Number of Proposal | Reader A's Score |
|---|---|
|  |  |

# Your Own Grant Reading Workshop

## Recording Sheets *(cont.)*

Reader B, keep a record of the scores you decide to give to each grant proposal you read.

| Number of Proposal | Reader B's Score |
|---|---|
| | |

# Your Own Grant Reading Workshop

## Recording Sheets *(cont.)*

### Compilation Sheet

Compile scores from Reader A's and Reader B's sheets. Compare their scores for each grant. If there is a discrepancy between grant proposal scores use a Reader C to decide a final score.

| Number of Proposal | Reader A's Score | Reader B's Score | Reader C's Score |
|---|---|---|---|
| | | | |

# Take the Test

## What Have You Learned?

Some of these questions are objective. Certainly, there has been a great deal of factual information to absorb so far. But, some of them are reflective. We all know by now that one of the best ways to take control of our learning is by reflecting on the progress we have made. So, here is your chance to be in charge.

1. What is the *narrative* in a grant proposal?

   _____

   _____

   _____

   _____

2. Why are they called RFPs (Requests For Proposals)?

   _____

   _____

   _____

   _____

3. Have you reached a new comfort level with the idea of reading grant material? Why or why not?

   _____

   _____

   _____

   _____

   _____

   _____

# Take the Test

## What Have You Learned? *(cont.)*

4. What does the word *"needs"* mean in grant terms?

_____

_____

_____

_____

5. What are *goals?*

_____

_____

_____

_____

6. What are *objectives?*

_____

_____

_____

_____

7. What are *activities?*

_____

_____

_____

_____

# Take the Test

## What Have You Learned? *(cont.)*

8. What is an *abstract?* What other names does it have?

_____

_____

_____

_____

9. What are *matching funds?*

_____

_____

_____

_____

10. What is *dissemination?*

_____

_____

_____

_____

11. What are some reasons you might want to write a grant proposal?

_____

_____

_____

_____

# Take the Test

## What Have You Learned? *(cont.)*

12. What could you do if you wrote a grant that did not get funded?

_____

_____

_____

_____

13. Do you think you might organize a Grant Committee at your school? Why or why not?

_____

_____

_____

_____

14. Which part of a grant proposal do you think is hardest to write?

_____

_____

_____

_____

15. Why do you think community partnerships are encouraged to apply for grants?

_____

_____

_____

_____

# Take the Test

## Annotated Answer Key

1.  The *narrative* in a grant proposal is just a term for the "story" you are writing. Unless there is a separate, special place for one of the elements that is called for in a grant, they all become part of the narrative. Often, when the grant separates its requirements into sections, the subtitles for the sections are simply chapters in the narrative.

2.  This is one of those answers that should really read, "Your guess is as good as mine!" However, one possible explanation is that many funding agencies and foundations like to say that they do not accept unsolicited grant applications. When they send out a Request For Proposal (RFP), they can attract proposals without breaking their own rule.

3.  It is to be hoped that you have reached a new comfort level, a *higher* one preferably. All of that paging through applications and guidelines must have helped a little. All those definitions and activity sheets must have helped too. Now, you are not uncomfortable with grant material; you have become inured to it!

4.  *Needs* are problems as they exist in the present. A statement of needs is a problem statement. It is a description of the *is;* the way things are.

5.  *Goals* are broad, general statements of purpose. They are also called *vision statements* or *mission statements*. They are not expressed in measurable terms.

6.  *Objectives* are outcome statements for the learner. They are written in measurable terms. They tell *who, what, when*, and *by how much*. They are a description of how things will be; the Should in contrast to the Is.

7.  *Activities* are methods, methodologies, or strategies. They are the things that you plan and do in order to move from the Is to the Should. Activities are really the things that you do every day in your classroom, whether or not you are applying for a grant.

8.  An *abstract* is also called a summary or a synopsis. It is a one page summation of your grant proposal. Abstracts are always required for federal grants and are sometimes used as screening devices.

9. *Matching funds* are funds which you acquire from another source to equal the amount of money you are requesting from the grantor. Various granting agencies and foundations have their own rules for matching funds. The one rule held in common seems to be that the applicant cannot supply them.

10. *Dissemination* means the process of spreading around or scattering broadly, like a farmer sowing seed. In a grant, it is the plan you have for sharing what you have learned and accomplished.

11. Have you thought of any reasons you might want to write a grant proposal? Well, there is always the obvious one—the money. But why do you need the money? You need it to help kids, to develop innovative curriculum, and to put your individual stamp on your profession. These, too, are valid reasons for writing grant proposals.

12. Perhaps, after you pick the pages of your proposal up off the floor, you would say, "Well, that's that. I tried and I failed. I'm through with grant writing." That is an understandable reaction, of course, but there are more practical responses. You could put it away and submit it again next year. (Maybe they ran out of money.) You could add some data and rewrite a little bit here and there. (Maybe they will like it better that way.) Or, you could take everything you learned, start from scratch, and write a new one. (Practice makes prefect!)

13. Some schools are ripe for the formation of a Grant Committee. Everyone is full of energy and looking for something new to do. Some schools are not. Maybe everyone is already working too hard and there are too many programs in action. You know what is really going on in your own school. If this is not the time, you could do the exercises on your own and maybe others will catch your interest and enthusiasm.

14. Each person will have an individual response here. If you have never written a measurable outcome, objectives may seem very difficult. On the other hand, many people are repelled by budgets. (Get someone else to do the part you dislike the most.)

15. Community partnerships are the newest and trendiest thing in education, not just in grant applications. If your school has a community partnership arrangement with a business, there may be many advantages, from old computers and printers when they upgrade to matching funds when they are deciding to make a contribution that will help them with the IRS. Public relations are also well-served by community partnerships. It is like having a built-in booster club.

# Individual Grants and Miscellany

## Table of Contents

# Individual Grants

## Now That You Are in The Mood

### Write One for Yourself

If you are in the mood to write a grant proposal, why not give yourself the benefit of what you have learned?  Some day when you have a large block of time, if you go to the Reference Desk in a main library, the librarian will show you where to find several large, current volumes full of *Foundation Grants for Individuals*.  These are amazing books, indexed in various ways to help you find something that might be of interest to you.

### A Needle in a Haystack

Looking for an individual grant that "fits" is like looking for the proverbial needle in a haystack.  You might find one that sounds just like you, only to discover that it is restricted to descendants of Confederate soldiers living in New Zealand.  However, if you have the patience and the time to persevere, you can probably find one to start on.  Or, look at the funding sources on pages 238 and 239 in this book and send away for information.

### Grants for All Seasons

In general, the grants for individuals divide up into these categories: higher education (in which case they are usually called scholarships or fellowships), the arts, and activism of one kind or another (environmental activism is big right now).

### Not Always Financially Adequate

Unfortunately, the stipends or funding offered to individuals have not kept with the times.  While grants to education have become massive in many cases, probably because technology is so costly, grants to individuals have not increased.  Even though tuition costs have skyrocketed, a scholarship award for a higher degree may be a very small amount.  This is probably because many of them were established many years ago when a few thousand dollars was a lot of money.  So weigh the effort you will need to put into your application and the accountability you will incur before you invest too much of your own time.

# Individual Grants

## Contact Letters

Your first contact with a funding source for individual grants will probably be ⎯⎯⎯ is best to request a RFP through the mail instead of by FAX or e-mail because you will ⎯⎯ ⎯y receive a clear copy and all of the extra forms you need.

3600 Elm Street
Any Town, CA 90000

September 20, 1998


Ellen Jefferson, Executive Secretary
Michael Jones Trust, Inc.
200 Main Street
Any City, MA 01746


Dear Ms. Jefferson:

Please send a copy of your application guidelines to

**Mary Lou Brown
3600 Elm Street
Any Town, CA 90000**

I am enclosing a self-addressed stamped envelope for your convenience.

Sincerely,

# Individual Grants

## Letters of Proposal

### No Forms

If you find a government agency that is giving money to individuals, you will be filling out an application form, no doubt. However, a private foundation or trust will probably ask for a letter of proposal.

Here are some of the instructions from one such trust:

---

### Requirements for a Letter of Proposal

**Format:**

- ❖ typewritten on 8 1/2" x 11" (22 cm x 28 cm) white paper
- ❖ no longer than five pages
- ❖ include address and telephone numbers

**Scope:**

- ❖ Description of the project
- ❖ Amount of grant requested
- ❖ Qualifications of applicant

There is a statement of the trust's goals and several instructions about what not to send. Then there is this statement.

"Please note that proposals should be no longer than five typed pages and should contain accurate information as to the objectives, time schedule, outline of proposed activities, the qualification of the applicant, a detailed budget, and the amount requested."

### Sound Familiar?

You know how to do this! It is the same narrative without the form or the section headings. Just write a proposal narrative, leaving out the headings but retaining all of the content that has been requested in all of the grant applications we have studied. You should have a winner, if you have remembered to choose a funder whose philosophy agrees with yours.

---

# Transfer Your Writing Skills

## Degree Programs and National Boards

## Many Applications

There are many practical applications for the writing skills that you have developed while working through the exercises in this book. They can be transferred to a variety of other areas.

## Degree Programs

Many degree programs in colleges and universities award units for the successful completion of a portfolio that represents and, in some cases, takes the place of the usual class work for a course. These portfolio projects tend to be very complicated, with elaborated formatting instructions and extensive writing guidelines. In other words, putting together one of these portfolio projects is very much like applying for a grant.

## National Board for Professional Teaching Standards (NBPTS)

One part of the national teacher's test administered by the NBPTS consists of this type of a portfolio. The successful creation of the portfolio, together with the test administrated at various locations around the United States, is a requirement for certification by this nonprofit/nonpartisan organization which was established in 1987 for the purpose of strengthening the teaching profession.

The organization is governed by a 63 member Board of Directors, the majority of whom are teachers. Its philosophy is that teaching is the heart of education and the most important way to improve education is to strengthen teaching. Their goals are to establish rigorous standards, to assess and certify teachers, and to promote educational reform. Some states recognize this certification of teachers and others support it in various ways.

If you are interested in transferring your skills to this prestigious undertaking, contact the organization at the address below.

---

**National Board for Professional Teaching Standards (NBPTS)**

**6818 Zarzamora**

**San Antonio, TX 78224**

**1-800-532-1813**

---

# Funding Sources

## Of Interest to Teachers

**Apple Community Affairs**

20525 Mariana Ave.

Cupertino, CA 95014

(408) 996-1010

Education Grants Program

Call for recorded information about this program and dates for grant applications.

**National Endowment for the Humanities**

1100 Pennsylvania Ave. N.W.

Washington, D.C. 20506

(202) 606-8400

Public Information Office

Call for general information and application forms.

**National Science Foundation**

4201 Wilson Blvd.

Arlington, VA 22230

(703) 306-1210 (general grants information)

(703) 303-1670 (grants for education)

Call for information and application forms.

**Quaker Oats Foundation**

c/o Ms. Anne Blanton

Chicago Community Trust

222 N. La Salle St., Suite 1400

Chicago, IL 60601-1009

(312) 222-7377 (Foundation)

(312) 372-3356 (Chicago Community Trust)

Call the Chicago Community Trust for guidelines.

**Target Stores**

Grants are handled through local stores. Call the store in your area and ask for the person who handles grants.

# Funding Sources

## Of Interest to Individuals and Women

| Of Interest to Individuals |
| --- |

**The Ella Lyman Cabot Trust**
109 Rockland Street
Holliston, MA 01746

Grants to individuals with projects that will contribute to and better the well-being of society.

**National Endowment for the Arts**
1100 Pennsylvania Ave. N.W.
Washington, D.C. 20506
(202) 682-5400

There are no more awards being made to individual artists.

Call for literature fellowships, guidelines, and application forms.

| Of Interest to Women |
| --- |

**The American Association of University Women**
1111 16th St. N.W.
Washington, D.C. 20036

Scholarships/fellowships to women for graduate study or advanced research.

**American Mensa, Ltd.**
Rita Levine Memorial Scholarship
2626 East 14th St.
Brooklyn, NY 11235

For women returning to school after the absence of seven or more years.

Send SASE for information/application.

**Business and Professional Women's Foundation**
2012 Massachusetts Ave. N.W.
Washington, D.C. 20036

Several scholarships.

Send SASE for information/application.

**Orville Redenbacher's Second Start Scholarship Program**
Box 4137
Blair, NE 68009

Send SASE for information/application.

**Society of Women Engineers**

Olive Lynn Salembler Scholarship
United Engineering Center, Rm. 305
345 East 47th St.
New York, NY 10017

Send SASE for information/application.

# Final Notes

## Publications, Bibliography, and Special Appreciation

### Publications

**Education Grants Alert**
(800) 655-5597

**Funding Update**
Education Funding Resources
11265 Canyon Drive
San Jose, CA 95127-1323
(408) 258-8020

**Grant Network Review**
Grant Research and Information
256 South Robertson Blvd., Suite 107
Beverly Hills, CA 90211
(213) 651-7368
e-mail: GrantNet@aol.com

**Grants for Schools**
Education Retrieval Resource
617 Wright Ave.
Terrytown, LA 70056-4037
(800) 891-6354

Write for free sample copy.

**GRANTS for School Districts Monthly Hotline**
(800) 229-2084

### Bibliography

Bauer, David G. *Grantseeking Primer for Classroom Leaders.* Scholastic, 1994.

Kiritz, Norton J. *Program Writing and Proposal Planning.* The Grantsmanship Center, 1980.

McKee, Cynthia Ruiz. "Financial Aid for Women." *New Woman.* September, 1992.

Nurnberg, Maxwell, *Questions You Always Wanted to Ask About English.* Pocket Books, 1972.

Strunk, Jr., William and White, E.B. *The Elements of Style.* Macmillan Publishing Co., Inc., 1979.

### Special Appreciation

Ellen Zimet, *EZGrants©*
9225 Ralph Street
Rosemead, CA 91770
(818) 573-3636 or FAX (818) 573-2772
e-mail EZGrants@aol.com